SHELDRAKE

MEMORIES OF A SECOND WORLD WAR GUNNER

SHELDRAKE

MEMORIES OF A SECOND WORLD WAR GUNNER

BY

MAJOR RICHARD HUGHES MC

Edited by Paul G. Hughes

Pen & Sword
MILITARY

In Loving Memory of
Richard and Rosemary Hughes

This book is dedicated to their Grandchildren,
Great Grandchildren, and their descendants:
Catherine, Suzie, Mark, Graham, Keith, Andrew, Matthew, Angelina,
Liam, Charlie, Isabella, Trevor, Natasha, Sean, Caitlin, Dylan, Evan

*'With the devout hope that neither you nor your families will ever have to
go through similar experiences.'*

Richard Hughes

This edition published in 2016 by

Pen & Sword Military
An imprint of
Pen & Sword Books Ltd.
47 Church Street
Barnsley
South Yorkshire
S70 2AS

ISBN: 9781473868601

A CIP catalogue record for this book is available from the British Library.

Printed and bound in England
By CPI Group (UK) Ltd., Croydon, CR0 4YY

Pen & Sword Books Ltd. incorporates the imprints of Pen & Sword Aviation, Pen & Sword Family History, Pen & Sword Maritime, Pen & Sword Military, Pen & Sword Discovery, Pen & Sword Politics, Pen & Sword Atlas, Pen & Sword Archaeology, Wharncliffe Local History, Wharncliffe True Crime, Wharncliffe Transport, Pen & Sword Select, Pen & Sword Military Classics, Leo Cooper, The Praetorian Press, Claymore Press, Remember When, Seaforth Publishing and Frontline Publishing

For a complete list of Pen & Sword titles please contact
PEN & SWORD BOOKS LIMITED
47 Church Street, Barnsley, South Yorkshire, S70 2AS, England
E-mail: enquiries@pen-and-sword.co.uk
Website: www.pen-and-sword.co.uk

CONTENTS

PREFACE
BY THE EDITOR

*R*ichard Hughes was an officer in the British Royal Artillery in World War II.

He was sent to the Continent twice. Initially he went as a reinforcement in 1940. But this assignment was short lived, as he was evacuated with the retreating British Army from the beach at Dunkirk.

He spent the next four years in rigorous intensive training throughout the British Isles.

In June, 1944, now a Major in command of a field battery, he participated in the Allied invasion of France. Over the next eleven months he fought in many battles right through Europe, to the cessation of hostilities in Germany in May, 1945.

Despite numerous close calls, he emerged unscathed.

Richard Hughes was my father. He left an excellent, detailed account of his wartime experiences in his personal journal. That is the heart of this volume. My motivation for publishing his memoirs is that I believe it is a valuable and interesting story which should be read by his grandchildren and their families.

I have attempted to make his text more reader-friendly, through simplification and removal of some technical jargon. However, as far as possible I have tried to keep the account in his own words. I have resisted the temptation to rewrite his text into what is supposedly the politically correct language of today. I do not believe I have the authority to do that.

Being typically British, Hughes reveals little of his own emotions in battle in these records. Indeed, although he frequently recounted stories of his war over the years, he spoke very little of what he actually felt. Was he afraid? Did he feel guilt, anger, hate, sorrow? We have to use our own imagination. Again, I have refrained from adding any embellishments which were not in his original text.

All we do know is that he was responsible for neutralising large numbers of the enemy – who, in turn, were equally intent on killing his infantry, his gunners, and himself. He was ordered to do a job, and he did it with typical vigour and efficiency.

His is a record of which we can be proud.

Paul Hughes

INTRODUCTION
BY THE EDITOR

*T*his introduction will attempt to describe, for the layman, the scenario within which Major Richard Hughes, Royal Artillery, played his role in Europe.

The War in Europe

After Hitler came to power in 1933 Germany invaded several neighbouring countries. When Hitler's forces annexed Poland, Britain gave Germany an ultimatum to withdraw. On 3 September, 1939, the ultimatum having been ignored, Britain declared war on Germany.

British forces were sent into Europe, and together with French and other European armies they fought the vastly better prepared Germans. By May, 1940, the Allies had been overwhelmed and driven back to the Channel. Despite a huge German onslaught, some 300,000 troops were evacuated from the beaches at and around Dunkirk, many taken off by an armada of small British boats which had braved the English Channel and enemy action to assist in the rescue.

So by mid-1940 Britain stood alone, with the entire European continent occupied by Germany and its allies. Three critical events followed, which paved the way for Germany's eventual loss of the war.

Through the summer of 1940, Germany threw the might of its airforce, the Luftwaffe, at Britain. A small number of young British and colonial pilots, whose life expectancy at that time was measured in hours, flew their Spitfire and Hurricane fighters with great skill and courage to defeat the Germans.

Secondly, having lost supremacy in the air, Hitler abandoned his planned 1940 invasion of Britain. From that time onwards, a seaborne invasion became less of an option as Britain gained in strength.

The third pivotal event was the Japanese attack on the US fleet at

Pearl Harbour, Hawaii, in December, 1941. This resulted in America entering the war on the side of the Allies, assuring them of eventual victory.

During the four years after Dunkirk, the Allies regrouped, built up their resources and trained mercilessly. By 1944 they were ready to invade and liberate Europe. That event came as 'D-Day', on 6 June, 1944. The Allied armies landed in Normandy, secured a foothold, then fought the Germans right through Europe to their final surrender near Hamburg in May, 1945.

The Infantry

The fundamental figure in an army is the Infantryman – the foot-soldier, the man on-the-ground, who is at the front line, fighting the enemy in trenches, fields, woods, and streets. The Infantry is supported by many other functional groups, such as Tanks, Engineers, Supply, Medical, Artillery, and so on.

This story follows the 2nd Battalion The Monmouthshire Regiment, an infantry battalion in the 53rd Welsh Division of the British Army. The battalion, known as 'The Mons' and described as such in this text, comprised some 1,000 officers and men. It was divided into four Infantry Companies, termed A, B, C, and D Company, each of around 100 men and under the command of a Major. The Companies, in turn, were divided into three Platoons of some 30 men. The Commanding Officer of the battalion was a Colonel – initially, Lt. Col. Walter Kempster, then, for the major part of this story, Lt. Col. Frank Brooke.

The Guns

The Artillery was deployed to support the Infantry. They were responsible for large guns – larger than the infantry would manage themselves. These field-guns had a range of several miles. They would be formed up behind the infantry, and could fire over their heads into enemy positions.

In 20th century ground warfare, shellfire was responsible for far more enemy casualties than any other type of ordnance.

Major Hughes was the Commanding Officer of 497 Battery, 133rd Field Regiment of the Royal Artillery. This battery was assigned to support The Mons throughout the 1944-45 campaign in Europe, and it was integral with the infantry battalion at all times.

497 Battery operated eight field-guns, known as 25 Pounders. These guns were versatile and mobile, had a bore of 3.45″ and a range of some 7 miles. They could fire a wide variety of ordnance, at rates of 6 to 8 rounds per minute. A crew of six fired each gun, and the total complement of the battery was some 200 men. Although the 25 Pounder was a comparatively small weapon, the rate of fire, the devastation it caused, and the speed at which it could respond had many German soldiers wondering if the British had developed an automatic field gun!

The Battery Tactical HQ (abbreviated as 'Tac') was typically based in a Half-track, a carrier with normal front wheels and tank-like tracks at the rear for cross-country grip. Tac would normally move in battle together with the infantry tactical command vehicle, Battalion HQ, at or near the front line. To obtain artillery targets, the Battery Commander would designate an Observation Post ('OP'). This would typically be within the infantry front line, in a tracked carrier, or in a suitable vantage point such as a tall building. The OP would be manned by a battery Forward Observation Officer ('FOO'), who would radio target coordinates and direct fire instructions back to the guns.

From time to time, targets might require more specialised artillery than the general-purpose 25 Pounder. Within the Regiment there were Medium and Heavy Batteries, with larger guns and specialised ammunition. If these resources were needed, the Battery Commander could call for fire support from them directly.

Major Hughes and the 497 Field Battery travelled and fought alongside The Mons from the invasion of France, through Belgium, Holland, and Germany, to Hamburg at the end of hostilities. He was in constant contact with Battalion Command, was involved in formulating the strategy for each battle and advance, and frequently took on the duty of Forward Observation Officer, personally directing the fire of his guns.

The Title

In the 1930s radio, or 'wireless' as it was called, was quite primitive, suffering from interference, lack of range, jamming, poor reliability, and so on. It was however an absolutely essential requirement for warfare.

The British Army developed a wireless 'language' of code words, which was designed to minimise misunderstanding and achieve quick and efficient communication in battle.

'Sheldrake' was the British Army wireless code for the senior artillery officer present at the called location. If the infantry needed artillery support they would radio call, ask for 'Sheldrake' and supply map coordinates. Sheldrake would then bring his guns into action in their support.

Major Hughes' individual wireless call-sign was 15C, spoken as 'One-Five-Charlie'. This became his nickname amongst his infantry comrades.

PART 1

A FORTNIGHT IN FRANCE

1939-1944

CHAPTER 1
THE BEGINNING

*W*ith some excitement, I watched the French coast appear out of the dawn. It was the morning of 10 May, 1940 – the day the Blitzkrieg started. But, let me take you back to the beginning.

At school, I was a member of the Officers Training Corps, and was commissioned as a 2nd Lieutenant into the 11th London Regiment, Territorial Army, in June, 1933. This was an Infantry regiment, but was later converted to Royal Artillery.

By 1937, parades and camp were taking too much of my time and interfered with my work. I therefore went on to the Reserve of Officers.

On 3 September, 1939 war was declared. I married my long-time girlfriend, Rosemary, and awaited mobilisation. This came in January, 1940.

I was ordered to report for training in Llandrindod Wells, Wales. Boarding the train with me at Paddington Station was a large contingent of reservists of all ages. One fact was common to us all. No one knew what awaited us in Llandrindod Wells. During the journey, speculation grew wild – were we Anti-Aircraft or Infantry, or what?

We arrived at the quiet little town, a holiday resort. It was quite unready for an invasion by hundreds of soldiers – the pubs did not even open on Sundays! Our speculation ended – we were all going into training to become Field Gunners. After checking in and assembly, we were allotted to various hotels in the town.

Then commenced the work of teaching us the difference between a gun and a howitzer. They may look similar but are quite different. A gun shoots low and very far, whereas a howitzer shoots high over shorter ranges, to get at enemy who are dug-in.

In those days, a Field Regiment was made up of two Batteries. Each Battery had two troops of field guns and one of howitzers. This

Lt. Richard Hughes, 1940.

arrangement led to difficulties in France where, in the heat of battle, each battery had to be supplied with two types of ammunition.

A solution to this problem was devised. Already a gun was in production which would serve as both gun and howitzer – the 25 Pounder Mk 2. There was only one issue, nobody had them yet! However the 25 Pounder was to be the subject of our study.

For the next two freezing months, we practised gun drill – using a chair and a broomstick – wandering over the frozen countryside, map-reading and theoretically laying out a gun position. All good things come to an end, and in March we were all sent to the School of Artillery at Larkhill on Salisbury Plain, except for two fellows who were held back to repeat the course.

At Larkhill we were to learn to shoot, but soon found out that the biggest menace was the gunnery instructors. Their furious outbursts were quite unbelievable. In retrospect, one must have sympathy for them. They were confronted with large numbers of green officers, all decked out as artillery (some probably thought they were still in infantry), but who were totally ignorant of their trade. And so they taught us what a gun looked like, and how to load and fire it. Then we went up forward to the Observation Post, to see what it was like when the shells landed.

After this session was completed we were sent to Ascot, where we carried out all sorts of manoeuvres on and around the race track for several weeks.

We had all come to the conclusion that the 'phoney war' would eventually be called off. Suddenly came great excitement – the Reinforcement Draft, of which I was a part, would be equipped and made ready to embark for the war!

Full of anticipation, we trooped down to the quartermaster stores to get:

Revolvers	None Available
Compasses	None Available
Binoculars	None Available
Battle Dress	None Available

We did get some webbing, a gas mask, and a tin hat each!

Somewhat deflated, we returned to the office. We were given travel warrants and told to go on embarkation leave.

On our return to Ascot, we were sent to Southampton to sail for France. Fully armed with swagger canes, we prepared to take on the apparently dozy Hun!

CHAPTER 2
A FORTNIGHT IN FRANCE

*B*eing my first excursion outside Britain, it was indeed with some excitement that I watched the French coast appear out of the dawn on that May morning.

Mystery Tour

Hugging our valises, we stepped out on to the landing stage at Le Havre. Our orders were to dump our gear at the railway station, then spend the day in town. We should return to the station at about 1900 hours, and then entrain to go to the Reinforcement Depot. We boarded, and after a long wait the train pulled out. We had no idea where we were going. Everything was dark – trains, stations, houses, and towns.

We pulled up at a halt in the early dawn. There was a mad dash to a pump at the end of the platform, as we were all parched. There had been no provision for meals or refreshments.

Later on the train arrived at a marshalling yard. I think it was Arras, but could have been Lille – it was a large town, but all the signs had been covered up.

Here we saw our first air-raid. The bangs and puffs of smoke from the anti-aircraft fire were, at first, very exciting. After a while the Huns flew away. There were no bombs or signs of damage. Everything became quiet and peaceful again, and the town's inhabitants returned to their normal occupation.

Our train rolled on again. The weather was glorious – clear blue sky and warm sun. We came to a stop at a small station, deep in the country – the name again blacked out for security reasons. The village boasted one café and two shops!

After alighting from the train, we dumped our kit and were marched to a nearby tented camp. The villagers were all very amicable

– 'Les Boches' were a long way off. No one had a radio, so we were all blissfully ignorant of what was going on. We stayed in this camp for a day or two, during which a lot of German planes flew over but did no harm.

One day, probably about 16 May, we were told that posting orders had arrived. We must go to the transit centre for our onward transport. We walked for several miles with a guide. At one point, we crossed an airfield with a dog-fight going on overhead. Planes, both Allied and Boche, fell like leaves, landing with huge firey explosions. We pushed on and eventually arrived at the depot.

Field Battery – French Village

I found that I was to join 24th Field Regiment, 48th Division, Royal Artillery. A truck took some of us into the night, and eventually stopped. My name was called and I got out. There were many flashes and bangs close by. Where I was, I never discovered.

I was guided into the Battery HQ, where a meal was produced. I was introduced to the Battery Commander and duty officers, who were all very busy because shooting was in progress. There was very little I could do, so I spread out my sleeping bag and tried to rest.

At daylight everyone began to move, but not a great deal was happening. The battery was in a village from which all the inhabitants had fled. Every home was abandoned, and each had been thoroughly looted. All drawers had been pulled out and the contents strewn about the floors. I wandered around, looking with a stranger's eye, and wondered who had done the pillaging. Was it troops, or others? A lot of people, as well as soldiers, had passed through. It is interesting to note that when I went back over the ground again in 1944/45, exactly the same state of affairs prevailed. It seemed endemic with evacuation and occupation. No sooner had the tenants left than some other party would go in to root for anything left behind.

On the main road, there was a steady stream of refugees. This was a great problem for the Army as, at that time, the refugees were going in the opposite direction. There were trucks and cars, horse-drawn carts, and hand carts all blocking the road and unwilling to give way. In addition, the German airforce regularly flew up and down, strafing the columns and causing more confusion and delay.

As our village was not on the main road, very little traffic came through. I saw one car which tried to use a side road as a bypass. It was heavily overloaded, packed with people and baggage. On the roof were tied boxes and mattresses. All this brought the vehicle down on its springs. As it bumped its way down the completely unmade road, it went over a hummock and knocked off the drain plug from its fuel tank. The family had no way to catch the leaking petrol. They could do nothing but stand and watch their only means of escape soak into the ground! Supplies of fuel and repairs were nonexistent by then.

The Battery Commander took me around the gun positions, and on the way back we heard some sad news. One of the troop commanders, driving down a narrow lane, met a German tank head-on. The tank opened fire, killing him and destroying his 8 cwt wireless truck. This was their first casualty. Apart from the shock was the sorrow – he was a very popular officer.

Holding the Fort

The next morning I was ordered to go to the Belgian Border to relieve a troop commander who was supporting infantry deployed in and around a pill box fortification.

The Battery Commander said, 'I am afraid there is no wireless available but we will try to run a telephone line out to keep you in touch.'

'Thank you, Sir', I replied.

'Well good luck, and by the way, the French Army will be taking over later on.'

I had heard that one before and, with due reservation, got into my truck.

'Go straight down to the border,' I said. 'I am told there is a pill box there.'

The driver made no comment but drove down through a village.

After a short while we found the pill box, and a Gunner captain whom I recognised.

He showed me around the facility. It was simply a concrete blockhouse up against an earth bank. The platoon of infantry were busy digging slit trenches outside. Inside it smelled damp. Over the door was an ominous notice – in English. It read:

'This post will be defended to the end. All men will remain here. If they cannot remain here alive, they will remain here dead.'

It was very cheering, but the fellow I was relieving said, 'As soon as the French arrive, you should just push off.' To this I was more than agreeable, but as yet, there was no sign of the French!

The Gunner captain showed me how to look outside the pill box, which was set close under a steep bank. There was a periscope. The vision was clear, but with one drawback – everything was upside down! It appeared that many hands had tried to assemble the periscope in the past. I filled in some hours fiddling with it, and had one last try. I pushed the viewfinder up its tube through the roof, and, what do you know? – the picture was the right way up, bright and clear, and also full of French soldiers led by an officer on a horse!!

This was good enough – as soon as they were in, I left and went to find the battery.

Chateau – Wormhoudt

On my return the Battery Commander said, 'There is another job for you. Take a motorcycle and go down to Brigade HQ in Wormhoudt. Report there as Regimental Liaison Officer.'

I found a motor cycle and also Brigade HQ, and made myself known. It was a cheery crowd in a lovely chateau.

Someone said, 'Come and eat!' We sat at a richly dressed table. The food and wine were excellent. There were no disturbances, and finally everyone got up to go to bed. I asked where I should sleep, and the Brigade Major said, 'There are lots of rooms upstairs.'

I found an empty one, and stretched out on a really comfortable bed. It was the last bed I would lie on until I was back in England!

In the morning, everyone got up. I went to the Brigade Major, who told me there was nothing for me to do there and that I should return to my unit.

Lucky Horseshoe – Ledringham

Shortly after my return the Battery Commander called me and said, 'There is another job for you. Go down to Ledringham. The Gloucesters are putting up a fight there. We do not have a wireless to spare, but we will try to get a telephone to you. Anyway see if you can be of any help.'

I found my regular truck and driver, and told him what we were up to. We followed the directions, via Wormhoudt, to the village of Ledringham. Quite clearly they were getting ready for a battle. I was directed to Battalion HQ, and walked through the door to hear the Colonel saying into a field telephone, 'Dig deep and secure! This may be our last stand!!'

He looked up, saw me, and said, 'A Gunner! Oh, Good!'

At this welcome, I found it impossible to spoil the illusion by saying, 'No guns – No wireless – Only me!'

At that moment there was no action in progress so I wandered outside – hopefully, to await the signallers with a telephone. It was plain that the Huns were coming. Along the hedgerow, about half a mile away, movement of their transport and infantry was clearly visible.

Another thing that the leading German troops did was to signal their position by firing Verey lights. We presumed they did this to let their aircraft and artillery know where the front line was, so not to shoot it up. Nothing like this was done in 1944–45. Presumably the Hun knew that if their position was so indicated, we would certainly shoot it up!

During the afternoon another troop commander appeared, fully equipped. He was a captain and a pleasant chap. He said, 'I'll take over here. You cannot do anything, so get back to your battery.'

I tried to demur but he repeated, 'Go back to your unit. We are going to be surrounded here very soon, so don't hang around. By the way, be careful on your way out – there are a lot of stray Huns creeping up behind us.'

With this caution, I got my truck and went in the general direction he had shown me on the map. It is of interest to note that the Gloucesters were surrounded, and that the captain who relieved me had to abandon his vehicle and equipment. He took up a rifle and bayonet, and fought his way out with the infantry. He was awarded the Military Cross.

We headed away from Ledringham towards Wormhoudt. There was a small cluster of soldiers at a crossing. I stopped to ask what was happening, and they said there was some noise and disturbance just ahead. Without much caution or common sense, I poked my head around the corner. Seeing the road apparently empty, I walked around.

A collection of farm horses appeared, and there was a burst of fire. It frightened the animals, which galloped towards me. I moved back into a doorway to get out of the way, and a horse threw a shoe, right in front of me. Thinking of good luck I bent to pick it up, but the shoe was nearly red hot and I dropped it. I bent again to retrieve the thing, and there was a burst of fire. There were several bullet holes in the door where I had just been standing! Hastily I withdrew, still gripping the shoe. It has now been hanging on the wall of my home for many years – for me a very lucky horseshoe!!

A Verey flare shot up from the road where this had taken place, so I decided a good thing would be to return to my truck and driver, and go somewhere else. Eventually we got back to the battery.

Retreat

After a night move backwards the Battery Commander said, 'The Colonel wants you to find a road to the beach.'

This was the first I had heard about a beach!

He gave me a piece of map, showed me where we were, near Killem, and told me to work out a route to the beach at Bray Dunes or La Panne. The Major said, 'Try to find a road not blocked or flooded. You will have to lead the regiment to the beach tomorrow morning.'

I got my truck and found the roads were cluttered with abandoned or shot-up vehicles. Some of the trucks were blazing after a recent air attack. Exploding ammunition made the going rather hazardous. Dead and wounded lay around, and medics were at work.

After some diversions and reconnaissance on foot, I found a usable route which was not yet choked. I returned to the battery and made my report.

At daybreak the regiment, or what was left of it, got on the move. I found to my satisfaction that I was able to recall and find the route, and also that it was still passable. The only complication was that the road was flooded on both sides, the dykes and locks having been broken. Finally we stopped not far short of the beach.

Next came the order to destroy and abandon everything. Vehicles, trucks, and guns were packed so close together that it was not practical to blow them up. All parts that could be removed were taken off and thrown into the water. The guns had their breech mechanisms dismantled, the recuperators exhausted, and then pushed into the flood as far as possible.

That done we moved on to the beach, just ahead.

The Beach

I was very naïve but, having had no real news for over a week, I could not believe what was happening.

There was no great surge of people to get to the beach – our track was so narrow that crowding was not possible. I took a last look at my valise and service dress (the battle-dress I was wearing had come from an abandoned depot). I packed a small haversack with shaving gear and a mess tin containing biscuits, cheese, and a Mars Bar. Then I wandered with the others on to the beach.

We were somewhere between Bray Dunes and La Panne. It seemed to me that there were not too many men when I got there. Everyone migrated towards people they knew. I spotted a subaltern from our battery and joined him. Nothing was organised. We saw a small café with the door open and went inside. We got coffee and fresh baked bread. There was no milk, butter or jam, but I was grateful for what we did get.

As soon as we were finished, we went outside. The weather was still

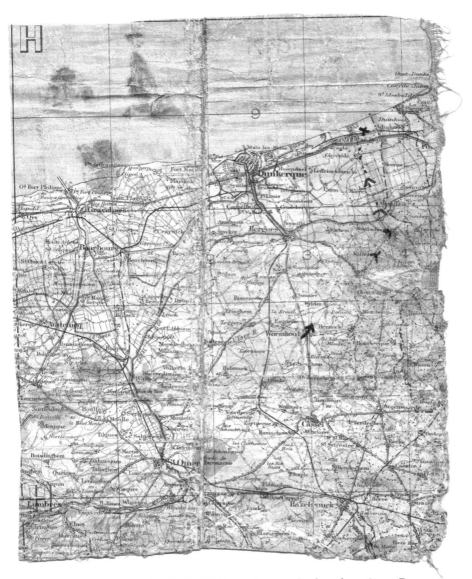

This piece of map led 24ᵗʰ Field Regt, RA, to the beach at Bray Dunes.

glorious, and our gaze turned towards Dunkirk. It was being heavily shelled and bombed, but for a while very little came our way.

There were no boats, and we wondered how we would leave – I don't think anyone gave serious thought to the alternative. I heard later that no boats would come to the beach until after dark – too many were being sunk.

Meanwhile there was nothing to do except wander around, collect as many of our soldiers as possible, and speculate on what would happen next. One thing did become apparent – as more troops arrived so did more shells. The patrolling Luftwaffe saw to that!

It seemed that few men had their small arms. I know that I had none when I arrived, nothing was issued to me, so I had none when I left. One valuable item that I had kept was my tin hat!

The day drew on, the noise from Dunkirk grew louder, but there was nothing we could do. No rations or food appeared. One of the fellows complained constantly of hunger, and I remembered the Mars Bar. Army biscuits had been my only food for two or three days, and every filling had come out of my teeth. The idea of eating a sweet Mars Bar was appalling, so I gave it to the hungry one – he was very grateful!

At dusk we began to settle down for the night. I borrowed a spade and dug a deep trench. It was warm, and felt safe as I looked at the stars – then I must have fallen asleep.

Some time later I was prodded awake, and a voice said, 'Will you lead this party of men to a boat?'

I climbed out of my trench and looked around in the darkness. I could make out five ships lying fairly close in, and small boats were at the beach. With a shout of, 'Follow Me!', I waded out. The boats were quickly filled, and rowed out to the waiting paddle steamers.

I climbed into the last rowboat, and was put off at the end steamer. On board I was directed to the saloon. Going into it brought a rush of nostalgia – memories of trips down the Thames on the Royal Eagle. I was first there, and a young ships officer said, 'Would you like a beer?' It was absolute heaven! I got the only one – there was none for the next two hundred or so who packed in.

After several hours, and some shooting outside, we moved off. I went out on deck – as we sailed along, it dawned the most glorious day. The sea was smooth, and eventually we were landed at Harwich.

Thus ended my first trip abroad – just two weeks!

CHAPTER 3
ENGLAND 1940-1944

*R*epatriation

As soon as we disembarked, we were entrained and taken to Leeds. I was billeted with a very hospitable couple. They had all the newspapers from the previous weeks, and from these I learned all that had happened.

Walking around the shops the following day, I met up with a number of chaps from our regiment, and gradually we collected together.

After a few days we were moved to Hereford. Some went into barracks. I was billeted with a wonderful couple, with whom we have now been friends for years. The husband was being called up for the Navy, and they wanted to go to see his family before he left. They asked if I would stay in their home while they were away, and maybe my wife might like to come down? Would she!!!! Yes, she did, and we had a wonderful reunion. Far too soon this idyll came to an end, and the regiment moved on again.

This time it was to Frome in Somerset, where more of our stragglers rejoined. The final move was to Doublebois, near Liskeard in Cornwall. We were being organised into a counter-attack force – in case of invasion!

For the next four years intensive training was the order of the day, either for the defence of Britain or ultimately for re-entry to the Continent of Europe.

132 Field Regiment

Shortly after our arrival in Liskeard I was promoted to Captain, and at the same time told that I, together with another officer, was being transferred to 132 Field Regiment in Rugeley, Staffordshire. 132 Field was a Territorial Unit, drawn largely from South Wales. With them training was continuous, in the course of which we went to most corners of the British Isles.

In 1942 I was promoted to Major, and given command of the battery with which I had trained for two years. This was gratifying – alas, it was not to last!

Our final move was to Stirling in Scotland, where the regiment was being refitted for active service.

One morning I was summoned by the Commanding Officer. The interview was brief. He told me it was no reflection on my work, but that the regiment would shortly be going into action overseas. The three majors were all fairly new and, as I was the newest, the Colonel felt he should have one with some seniority. Accordingly the chap I had succeeded was returning and I was being relieved of my command!

This was a numbing blow – after all this work, to come to nothing! I managed to ask, 'When do I leave?' The reply was 'Today!'

I was told to pack my gear, get a rail warrant, and go home. Then relenting a bit, the Second in Command, who was also a Major, realised the effect of what he was saying. He added, 'The Colonel is now in London, and has said he will do his best at the War Office to see that you will not lose by this. You will get another posting in due course'.

At times like this, when anger and disappointment are one's overwhelming feelings, it is always hard to understand the mysterious moves of Fate. At that moment there was no way I could foresee that this was probably the best thing that could ever have happened.

I left 132 and went home to my wife, who was expecting our first child. I stayed there for about six weeks.

One day, a War Office letter arrived. It contained orders to report to 133 Field Regiment at Maidstone, in Kent. I immediately phoned to ask what job I would get. The Adjudant answered, and it turned out that we knew each other. His reply filled me with joy! 'We are short of a Battery Commander. You are it! Your late Colonel gave you a good write-up!'

497 Field Battery*

The Adjutant met me at Maidstone and introduced me to the Colonel. He took me to meet the 497 Field Battery.

They were a friendly, helpful bunch of people, but they had had some rough treatment and were by no means efficient. There had been a lot of personnel changes, where men had frequently been taken for reinforcements elsewhere.

The battery consisted of eight 25 Pounder field guns and a complement of some 200 officers and men. We had a very useful and productive first meeting, and quickly got down to learning our job. We worked long and hard at polishing our skills. I assumed command of 497 Battery in 1942, and the team remained intact until the end of the war in 1945.

In 1943 we became part of the 21st Army Group. This meant that our division would be fully equipped to become part of the invading forces, commanded by Field Marshal Montgomery. The soldiers loved the idea!!

497 Field Battery, Royal Artillery, was at peak efficiency by June, 1944, when we went to war. Everyone worked well together, officers and men alike. The response from the guns was always fast, accurate, and deadly. That was not my assessment but that of those who relied on us for their protection – the Infantry.

* See Appendix 3 starting on page 157.

Officers of 497 Battery, 1943; Major Hughes and Captain David Thomson front right.

PART 2

THE SECOND FRONT

JUNE 1944 TO MAY 1945

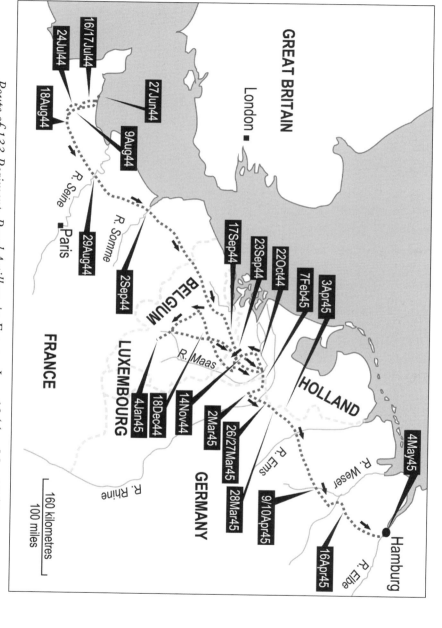

Route of 133 Regiment, Royal Artillery, in Europe, June 1944 to May 1945.

GREAT BRITAIN

London ■

24Jul44
16/17Jul44
27Jun44
18Aug44
9Aug44

R. Seine
■ Paris
R. Somme
29Aug44
2Sep44

BELGIUM

FRANCE

LUXEMBOURG

17Sep44
23Sep44
22Oct44
7Feb45
3Apr45

R. Maas

HOLLAND

4Jan45
18Dec44
14Nov44
2Mar45
26/27Mar45
28Mar45
9/10Apr45
16Apr45

R. Ems
R. Weser
R. Elbe

4May45

Hamburg

GERMANY

R. Rhine

160 kilometres
100 miles

36

CHAPTER 4
THE LANDINGS
27 JUNE TO 20 JULY 1944

*A*lmost exactly four years after the evacuation from Dunkirk I returned to France as Commanding Officer of 497 Field Battery. Our job was to provide artillery support to an infantry regiment, the 2nd Battalion the Monmouthshire Regiment, or as they were known to one and all, 'The Mons'.

The Landings

It was a beautiful day on 27 June, 1944 when the landing of the Battery took place. The beach at Arromanches shelved gently into the water, and a record of all vehicles safely ashore pleased everyone.

This was some three weeks after the D-Day Landings. As I looked around from the ship and later from the shore, I realised how violent the opening struggle had been. There were wrecked ships, bombed and smashed houses and debris everywhere. At the same time, the organisation that had gone into the landings was obvious from the amount of administration and structure to be seen. The Mulberry Harbour, brought in from England in huge floating concrete sections, was being assembled, although it was not yet working. Beach recovery and supply points were all signposted and well organised, and there were many other indications that we had come here to stay.

The Battery moved inland to get clear of the beach. We then pulled off the road to do the initial work of removing the waterproofing material from the engines, so the vehicles could be driven to the concentration area.

When ready and given permission by Traffic Control, we made our way up the dusty road into Bayeux. There were surprisingly few signs

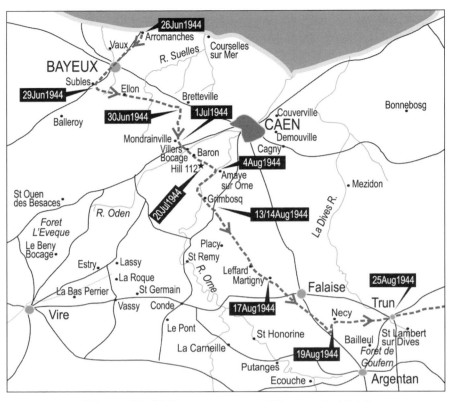

Moves of 2nd Mons regiment in Normandy 1944.

of battle in this area, and the French people were going about their business in an everyday manner.

Just outside Bayeux I saw the first grave. It was of a captain in the armoured corps. Although I did not say anything, the sight of this lonely grave by the side of the road brought home with a thump the realisation that this was war at last – the years of exercises were over. I have no doubt that it was not the first grave in the area but it was the first I had seen. I got the feeling of one about to sit in the dentist's chair, that feeling of entering the unknown and hoping that one would behave well.

We joined up with the rest of the regiment who were harboured, and spent the night 'dug in'. I put in the inverted commas because I had my bed dug down about 18 inches, and felt very safe. In the days that followed, we all learnt that anything less than three feet down and 18

Mondrainville; Our first OP was in this church tower.

inches of head cover was inviting trouble, and that you would not feel safe until you had three or maybe four feet on top!

The following day we were ordered to send an OP (Artillery Observation Post) to the forward infantry units.

Captain David Thomson (one of my FOOs, or Forward Observation Officers) and I went up to find The Mons. We located them at Le Mesnil-Patry (known by all as 'Mess in the Pantry'). We were greeting all our old friends when the CO, Colonel Walter Kempster, arrived. He called his group of officers into an orchard for briefing. As we assembled, a large and prolonged concentration of shells came down. This barrage brought The Mons their first casualties of the campaign.

Shortly after this there came a call for COs to Brigade HQ. We guessed that something was in the wind, but no orders came for me and I returned to the Battery.

Mondrainville

At this time, about three weeks after the invasion, the Germans were vigorously defending Normandy. Their elite forces were confronting the British and Canadian advance head-on in the area around Caen, with the aim of throwing us back into the Channel. Meanwhile the Americans were pushing forward around the German west flank, with the objective of encircling and trapping the enemy forces in what was to become known as the Falaise Pocket.

Evrecy from Mondrainville.

On 2 July I learned that The Mons, together with the rest of the infantry in the division, had moved into the front line at Mondrainville. This was just short of the River Odon and a few miles west of Caen. It was one of the hottest spots along the whole front, as retention of Caen was vital to the Germans.

Up to this time, the 15th Scottish gunners had been supporting The Mons. 497 Battery was ordered to relieve them the following day.

That evening Major Chessells, our Artillery 2nd in command, ordered Battery Commanders forward on a recce. It turned out that we would be expected to stay with our assigned infantry battalions on an ongoing basis, and not with our batteries. So from this point, I would travel and be located alongside The Mons Battalion HQ for the rest of the war.

I sent a hasty message to David Thomson to follow me, and drove up to meet the Scottish battery commander in my Jeep. He told me that The Mons had had a very rough first day. Their Battalion HQ had received a direct hit which killed their second-in-command and wounded several officers, in addition to several other casualties. I followed the battery commander down into the village of Mondrainville, where I was destined to spend the first shell-wracked fortnight of my campaign.

Major Hughes briefing Battery personnel in an orchard in Normandy.

On arriving at Battalion HQ I found that Jerry Weiss, an old friend, was adjutant. I spent the rest of an uncomfortable night with frequent bangs close by. David arrived at about 0230 after a bad journey.

When daylight came I went to the Observation Post (OP), which was set up in the ruins of a church, and looked across a scene of desolation. The ground swept away down to the River Odon about half a mile off. At the bottom of the slope was Gavrus, with its few houses all badly shelled. To our right was Granville, and to our left Caen. Beyond the Odon the ground rose very sharply and became woodland. Over the whole front, the Hun's presence was very evident, with transport, mortars, and tanks all being clearly visible.

Shells and mortars came down about every ten minutes for the first three days. However as our guns and an air OP became more organised, we commenced firing heavy retaliation and things eased up a bit. Although the enemy fire never ceased, we did get spells of an hour or two between incoming concentrations.

After about five days Colonel Kempster decided to move Battalion HQ. We shifted up the road about one quarter of a mile to another orchard, where we were again periodically shelled as a matter of routine.

About this time the Ox and Bucks Light Infantry put in a night attack on Cahier, near Le Valtru. The Huns were pretty good because, although they knew they were being attacked, they remained in their slit trenches until daylight, then opened up on our chaps from the rear. It was only after a long and heroic struggle that the Ox and Bucks achieved their objective. The following night we were ordered to relieve them. This we did without casualties, and we took a few prisoners.

A few days later we moved again, this time on to the River Odon. The usual shelling and mortaring continued as a fairly regular routine.

During all this period the weather had been very hot and, at times, sultry. As a result recces and journeys around the country were getting steadily more and more horrible with the stench of rotting flesh from dead cattle. They were impossible to bury under the circumstances.

After another few days we made a move through Baron, and went to relieve the 43rd Division on the now famous, or infamous, Hill 112.

CHAPTER 5
HILL 112
20 JULY TO 4 AUGUST 1944

*H*ill 112 was a very bare feature which ran up from the woodlands around the River Odon. The ground was solid chalk and very difficult for digging. Almost due west of Caen, it had unobstructed views to the Odon and Orne rivers and to the city of Caen. It was crowned by three woods, the biggest being known as Square Wood. These woods were but shadows of their former selves, having been cut down by shellfire which left only straggling trunks. Nevertheless they offered a very distinct landmark in an otherwise featureless scene. The Germans appreciated the importance of this vantage point, and were desperate to hold on to it at all costs.

The 5th Duke of Cornwall's Light Infantry (DCLI) of 43rd Division had had a very bad time in heavy fighting for this strategic location. They had lost so many men in the attack that the name 'Cornwall Hill' had been approved for this landmark.

The Mons were ordered to relieve the DCLI on 20 July, and we took over on a fine, sunny day. Two companies advanced well forward towards the top of the slope, and another to the right, also well up. The fourth company was held in reserve, and Battalion HQ was dug into the chalk at the foot of the slope.

Soon after we took over, a hate commenced and, as usual, this continued throughout our stay. The Battalion Pioneers did great work in helping us build our artillery dugout, and they put on a fine roof. This was a good job, as one night when I was sitting in there with the duty signaller we received a direct hit on the roof from a shell. Although we could see nothing for dust, nobody was hurt and no damage was done save for a bent sheet in the roof.

Hill 112. The DCLI lost 700 men here.
The nickname 'Cornwall Hill' was approved.

The Battalion fought at Hill 112 for about two weeks.

On 29 July The Mons carried out their first real assault against the enemy. It was known that in the small triangular wood to the left of Square Wood, there was a platoon of enemy. The objective of the raid was to ascertain the identity of the opposing troops, and to bring back a prisoner if possible.

The plan was to put down a very heavy barrage, then launch D Company into the wood with two Wasps (carriers with flame throwing apparatus mounted on them). The operation went exactly as planned. The fireplan stunned the enemy, and D Company went in with the flamethrowers which got the Hun out of his slit trenches with his hands up. The total bag was the complete platoon, plus a German gunnery FOO (forward observation officer). Unfortunately one of the Wasps either got bogged or shed a track and had to be abandoned.

All was going to plan when tragedy struck. The enemy put down defensive fire which slightly wounded one of The Mons. My OP sergeant, seeing him in trouble, left his dugout to go and help, just as the next concentration arrived which unhappily killed them both.

Time on Hill 112 passed until about 3 August, when intelligence was received that the enemy might be pulling back. We did not believe it, but a patrol was sent to the top and, indeed, no enemy was there. A company was sent immediately to occupy the other side, and Colonel Kempster and I went up to have a look. From the top of the hill we could see the ruins of Esquay, Evrecy, Ferme de Mondaville, and other places where the fighting had been very intense. Also clearly visible in every detail were our first two Battalion HQs – no wonder the Hun gave us such a warm welcome!

Forward, one could see for miles, but there were few, if any, Hun as he had made a clean break and had pulled back to the River Orne. The hilltop and surrounding area was a veritable charnel house. The stench was dreadful. Corpses of Huns and our chaps lay around everywhere. Every ditch and slit trench was a shallow grave – far too shallow for hygiene.

The following day we were ordered to move forward to the River Orne via Amaye-sur-Orne, which we did without misadventure.

On 9 August we were saddened to learn that the Commanding Officer of The Mons, Colonel Kempster, was being transferred to 3rd Division, and he left the battalion immediately. Major Tyler temporarily assumed command.

About this time our second tragedy occurred when the Command Post Officer was on a recce for a new gun position. The accompanying truck backed into a gateway to turn around and blew up on a mine, which killed one and rendered casualty the whole crew. Shortly after this the CPO, Dick Gadd, collapsed and had to be evacuated to England. He had not been fit for some time and had been overworking.

The next 48 hours were quiet. Then, quite by accident, I met up with a patrol the Canadians had sent out to link up with us. What a handshake that was!

CHAPTER 6
BATTLE FOR LE LOGIS
14 AUGUST 1944

*E*arly in August, the cream of German forces were being encircled by the Allies in the Falaise Pocket. The Americans had broken through the western flank after the landings, and now came up behind the enemy from the south.

The next objectives for The Mons were a series of high-ground positions, which would command the countryside around Falaise and Argentan – namely Le Logis, Hill 210, and Leffard.

Orders came on 13 August for us to cross the River Orne, and move into action near Fresnay. We passed through the forest which had been the scene of very heavy fighting by 158 Brigade during the preceding 24 hours, and where Tasker Watkins of 5th Welch got his VC.*

We arrived in the afternoon, but there was no shooting to do except for a few harassing tasks and I spent a fairly quiet night with the Battery.

About 0830 hours I received an urgent call from the CO to move immediately with one OP (Observation Post) and join The Mons. He could give me no information except that they had commenced a battle, they were in trouble, and needed artillery assistance. Taking Captain David Salmon with me, I moved up to see what was happening. It was easy to find The Mons, as the transport and anti-tank guns were lined up along our axis, so we passed by the stationary column until arriving at Battalion HQ.

A general description of Le Logis is useful at this point. The village consisted of just three farms in an area about half a mile square, with a minor road running through the middle. It lay in a hollow with woods all round, so that any observation was extremely difficult. Our approach road ran through a thick wood, the edge of which was some 500 yards

Major Hughes with an OP carrier and crew.

short of the top of a rise beyond which lay the village. Along this crest ran a main road at right angles to our path. As soon as one reached the main road Le Logis suddenly came into view.

Battalion HQ was situated at the edge of the wood. When I arrived I was told that the acting CO, Major Tyler, had gone forward so I followed in his direction. It was pretty uncomfortable because, not only was the enemy mortaring the area very thoroughly, but also a considerable amount of small arms fire was coming over the crest and dropping all around. Two carriers were burning fiercely on the crest and two armoured cars from our Recce Regt were knocked out.

I must have missed the CO somehow, because I went right up and over the crest without meeting him. As soon as I crossed the horizon I became a target, and took cover in a slit trench. This, to my horror, was already occupied by a Hun who presumably did not know his war was over! An amicable agreement was quickly reached. He got out and ran back to our lines with his hands up. As soon as I saw he was not shot I did the same, and very quickly too!

On arriving back at Battalion HQ, the CO put me in the picture. Three companies had intended to advance and occupy the centre of the village under cover of a fireplan. Unfortunately the advance by B Company was slower than expected. The fireplan had ended before they had reached their objective, and they had been forced to go to ground near the first farm. A Company had got about half way to their objective when the Hun, now thoroughly aroused, had pinned them down with Spandau fire and fire from a Panther tank in one of the farm buildings. C Company was still manoeuvring but could do little to help. The Hun was using mortars from the village, but it was impossible for me to help owing to the proximity of A and B Companies to the enemy.

Casualties were coming back very fast, and it was obvious that a new approach would have to be devised. I sent David Salmon to look for an OP site, but he returned after an hour saying that observation without going on to the forward slope was impossible. About this time the CO was called to Brigade HQ, and all we could do was sit and wait. This was very unpleasant knowing the hell that the two forward companies were receiving.

Eventually the CO returned to report that a fresh fireplan had been made together with the CO of 81st Division, and he gave me the details. At 1800 hrs we would attack from the extreme right with C and D Companies, to be supported by two squadrons of Churchill tanks.

At about 1630, B Company reported that they were being attacked by the Panther tank. It had been hidden in the farm, but now drove forward until it was nearly on top of them. Fortunately it could not depress its gun far enough to harm them, and they fired PIATs (anti-tank weapons) at it until it withdrew up the road. As a matter of interest it withdrew into the 6th Royal Welsh Fusiliers, who had intersected the road further up. They finally killed it with another PIAT.

The fresh attack was launched on schedule and provoked some enemy defensive fire, a shell of which fell into my party and tragically killed my half-track driver, Sgt. 'Snowy' Davis. The attack was quite successful. The Mons got right in and cleared the village, taking some 35 prisoners

25-pounder in action.

and finding a satisfactory number of dead Huns. But the cost to us had been significant.

I radioed back to David Thomson, who was acting Battery Captain, to bring up a replacement driver. Then we awaited the arrival of 71st Brigade, who were to pass through us when the road was cleared.

David had barely arrived with a new driver, when Brigadier Blomfield, Commander of 71st Brigade came up and informed our CO that we were to continue under his command, and advance to take Hill 210.

It was hard to break the news of Sgt. Davis' death to my jeep driver as they were very great buddies. However Gunner Harris took it well, and when I asked him to take over driving the half-track which he had never driven before, he readily agreed and was my driver for the rest of the war – through thick and thin he never faltered.

Lt Tasker Watkins was the first Welshman to be awarded a VC (Victoria Cross) in World War II. His company was pinned down by heavy machine-gun fire. After all the other officers were killed, he led the remnants of his company on a bayonet charge against 50 enemy. Then he single-handedly took out a German machine-gun post, and brought his men back to safety. His superb leadership decisively influenced the course of the battle.

A prominent personality, Watkins later became a Lord Justice of Appeal, and also President of the Welsh Rugby Union. He was knighted in 1990. (Ed)

CHAPTER 7

THE INCIDENT ON HILL 210

14 AUGUST 1944

*B*eyond Le Logis the ground rose fairly steadily for about a mile and a half, dropped into a valley, and then rose steeply to a crest. This crest was Point 210, our next objective. The road from Le Logis was winding in most places and enclosed by hedges and trees. There was little sign of movement on the ground in front, but eyes were obviously watching our every move.

After the Brigadier had left us in Le Logis, the CO ordered C Company to lead the way, followed by D Company, at the head of which would be Battalion HQ. I therefore ordered David Salmon to go with C Company, whilst I followed in the usual place behind the CO with my half-track. Along the first part of the road we went through the 6th Royal Welsh Fusiliers, and saw ample evidence of the energy they had put into their part of the job from numerous corpses and burnt out vehicles.

All looked very quiet when we came in sight of our objective. I found it in my heart to hope that the Hun had really gone right back, and that we should have a peaceful occupation. C Company moved steadily ahead, followed by Battalion HQ. We saw their leading platoon disappear over the top, then there was a burst of small arms fire and a sudden call over the radio from the company commander for an artillery target. I started to deal with this as we reached the bottom of the valley, when suddenly heavy firing broke out all around Battalion HQ. We had walked into an ambush! Also, being at the bottom of the hill meant that I lost wireless communication back to the Battery. Another frantic call came from C Company for their target, and in a moment of clarity on the air my operator got it through.

Battery Commander's half-track, 'X', in the woods.

All this time a brisk firefight was in progress at close quarters. In calling for the target, I asked for the whole regiment scale 5. But due to the local struggle I had not realised a mistake had been made in the map reference – in fact C Company had asked for the fire to fall on their own position. As we were only a hundred yards or so away, this meant that some would fall on Battalion HQ as well.

The small arms fire around us died away as the Boche gave up, but then they mortared us in the valley, which was nasty.

Then down came our regimental concentration. I had not been able to get a 'Stop' through to the guns as the wireless was still jammed. I was putting the Bren gun back in the half-track when our shells arrived. As I started to jump out a round hit the side, flames seemed to come through every crevice and I hit my head and lost all interest in the proceedings. On coming to, I saw Harris stretched out behind the steering wheel and I thought he had been hit. We dragged him out and were very relieved to find that he was mainly winded, having been thrown against the wheel.

Bombardier Harris cooking beside 'X'.

As a result of the general filth that had descended, the CO decided that Battalion HQ could not get on top of the hill and should pull back a few hundred yards up the road behind us until things settled down. This we did, but on approaching the top were suddenly taken on by an 88 mm gun further along, into whose field of vision we had emerged. This was very unpleasant and we took some casualties, but after we retaliated with some fifty rounds it stopped and we completed our withdrawal under cover.

A bath in the woods. Note the shower!

By this time C and D Companies had got on to their objectives, and after making the position fairly secure we reported what had happened and awaited orders for the next move.

CHAPTER 8
THE BATTLE FOR LEFFARD
15 AUGUST 1944

*A*t 0430 hours orders came to push forward, clear the road of mines and obstructions, and locate the enemy. But under no circumstances were we to get involved in a battle. This seemed a job right up our street under the circumstances and so, on a beautiful August morning, we moved off. D Company was in the lead and David Salmon went with them as FOO (Forward Observation Officer).

Mines were found scattered about on the road and duly lifted, but there was no sign of Boche for about two miles. Then the leading patrol reported resistance at Leffard, another small village on our axis. The Mons prodded at them with a fighting patrol but there was no sign of them giving way, so the CO reported to Brigade that we had come up against enemy resistance. We then awaited 158 Brigade (E. Lancs), who were to pass through us and clear the road.

Nothing exciting happened for some hours except for a couple of mortar concentrations, which holed the radiator of my half-track and drove us underground.

At 1500 hours Brigade sent for the CO. He returned in an hour to inform us that we were now under command of 158 Brigade, and that we ourselves would attack and clear the village of Leffard. As soon as that was done, 158 Brigade proper would advance through us. The attack would go in at 1700, a fireplan had been laid on, and a squadron of Crocodiles (flame-throwing Churchill tanks) would support the action.

At 1655 hours the fireplan started but the Crocodiles had not arrived, so the attack went in without them. There was significant resistance and heavy fighting. Then the enemy appeared from slit trenches and behind walls with their hands up, holding smoking rifles and shouting, 'Don't shoot! Me Polski' or 'Me Ruski', meaning they were Poles or Russians forced to fight for the Germans. This yarn impressed us at first, but it soon wore thin when we saw how hard they fought until we got up to them. According to a Russian officer who visited, they were in for a tough time on their return to Russia!

There was some sniping, then reports came in from all Companies that they were on their objectives. After clearing the immediate area about 120 prisoners were taken, all pretty shaggy and tired, most from horsedrawn or infantry units.

The situation seemed well in hand, and Battalion HQ was set up temporarily in a shop in the village centre. A message was sent to 158 Brigade advising that Leffard had been cleared. Then the CO went forward to talk to C Company, taking his driver and dispatch rider as escorts.

As we stood by the roadside, all extremely weary, the welcome sight of the leading Battalion of 158 Brigade came in sight. The first part went through and, just as their Battalion HQ came level with ours, a terrific burst of Spandau and heavy machine gun fire started, all very close to us. A breathless runner told us that a big counter attack was on its way.

My half-track was parked partly under cover and I had hung my headset and microphones on the side rail in the open. I dashed to get them, and as quickly dashed back as a well-aimed series of sniper's bullets hit the side about three inches from my hand!

To complete the confusion, the CO's dispatch rider came running in to say that the CO had been ambushed, and was either a casualty or had been captured.

The Battalion of 158 Brigade proceeded to take up a defensive position until we could work out what was happening. Then, to our relief, a very breathless and scratched CO walked in with some explanations. Apparently after he had gone forward about 200 yards, some 70 Boche surrendered to him. He started to drive them on towards C Company when another party of about ten appeared. He called on them to surrender, but they replied with bullets and attempted to rescue those he was already escorting. In the melee his driver was shot and killed, and his dispatch rider made a speedy return to Battalion HQ.

The other confusion was from a party of about thirty Boche who had been bypassed during our advance. As soon as they saw us they let fly with all the automatic weapons in their possession. Most of this party eventually surrendered, but it was a very uncomfortable feeling for us as we did not know how many more were out there in the thick woods.

As I had been cut off from my own (artillery) CO for over 48 hours, I decided to go to see him and collect rations en route. When I started down the road in my jeep a sniper had another couple of shots at us – later we found he had shot away the cover of the spare wheel. After meeting with the CO I made my way back to The Mons, and found everyone still rather fidgety in a black night waiting for dawn.

About 0400 hours, 158 Brigade started to move forward. By 1000 there were corps and divisional trucks passing through, and it was hard to believe that only twelve hours previously the battle for possession of Leffard had been raging.

The following day we joined up with our brigade again, and started the push through towards the Falaise – Argentan road, in the combined effort to trap the German army in the Falaise Pocket.

CHAPTER 9
NECY – TIGER CORNER
19 AUGUST 1944

The next objective was to occupy the high ground south of the village of Necy. This was essential to close a gap in the ring surrounding the enemy in the rapidly contracting Falaise Pocket.

Our leading companies got to the Falaise – Argentan road before serious opposition was encountered and the Battalion and supporting elements all followed up.

It was a hot sunny day and very dusty. The Mons vehicles were passing me. As the CO's carrier went by a voice shouted, 'Hello, Dick!' The vehicle stopped and I ran across to welcome the new Mons Commanding Officer, Lt. Colonel Frank H. Brooke. He had just taken over the Battalion and I had known him when we trained together back in England.

As I shook hands and said how pleased I was to see him, we started on a partnership which was to last many months and come through many trying battles. Our relationship was never marred by a single cross word or difference of opinion, which made my job of artillery support much easier. No words of mine can express enough appreciation for the thoughtful consideration with which our guns were used. No FOO or artillery crew was ever unnecessarily risked. In fact, from that time onwards we only had one member of our OP parties killed – it may have been luck, but I am sure we owed a great deal to our Infantry Battalion Commanding Officer, Colonel 'Frankie' Brooke.

The guns went into action, and for the first time the command post was put into a house instead of being dug into the ground. The greater room and comfort was appreciated by all. Just after getting in our neighbouring battery, 331, was heavily shelled, with some killed and wounded. Fortunately my battery escaped.

Brigadier Frank H. Brooke, D.S.O., CO of The Mons
from August 1944 to April 1945.

At 1900 hours, Colonel Brooke was summoned to an Orders Group at Brigade HQ, and he asked me along. It was a hot sultry evening, and the brigade command tent was stifling. The Brigadier put Colonel

Brooke in the picture. Our troops held control all the way along the Falaise – Argentan road, with the enemy holding the other side. They were thought to be preparing to pull back up the one remaining road from the Falaise Pocket.

It was to be our job to cross the Falaise – Argentan road and push forward to Necy. The village commanded the last road junction they could use, and we were to seal it off. Necy lay some three miles into enemy country.

When the Brigadier had finished Colonel Brooke said, rather unhappily, that it seemed a risky procedure as Germans were all around the road we would use. But worse was yet to come – in a silence you could feel, the Brigadier said, 'You have to be there by first light.'

I will admit to being as horror struck as was Colonel Brooke. He got up, said 'Battalion Orders Group at 2100', and left. I then did something I had never done before nor since. I went back to the Battery, ordered David Thomson to make ready, and then gave instructions for the disposal of my effects and packed up, because I did not see how we could possibly survive. Leaving orders for David to follow me, I went off to the 'O' Group.

The CO decided on a policy of stealth. Everything that made a noise would be left behind, transport being confined to his carrier and David's, on which I should ride. The carrier platoon, the dispatch riders, the Lloyds, towing 6 pounders, would remain behind until called for, and Jerry Weiss would come up with my half-track.

At 0130 hours we moved off, and although it was a fairly light night, all was pretty ghostly. The main road stretched out, a white ribbon in front of us, and nothing moved except us. Apart from some banging away to the south, it was all very quiet. I admit getting into a rather nervy state, and the crunch of feet on the road and the soft restrained purring of the carriers seemed to raise echoes all around.

B Company was going ahead very well at a good speed in almost complete silence and causing no alarm. Then came the moment to leave the main road and advance into enemy country. We turned left down a very dark track, still with no sign of life. After a while we turned right over a railway bridge, and arrived at the little village of Necy itself. By this time we were on a sandy road and, to me sitting on top of the carrier, it seemed that we were kicking up a terrific row. I would have sold my soul for a cigarette, but that would have been too risky. Passing between a high wall on one side and a hedge on the other, one had the feeling that at any moment there would be a challenge or a shot – but no, not a sound.

There were a number of vehicles of various sorts parked around Necy, the type of impressed cars and trucks the Germans used for their lesser divisions. I whispered to David that they did not look badly smashed up, especially since the RAF and artillery had attended to the village. It never dawned on me that they did not look smashed because they had only been parked there about three hours beforehand, and that all the drivers and crews were sleeping in exhaustion in the surrounding houses.

We pressed on towards our objective, a junction about a mile past the village up the hedge-lined road. After what seemed an interminable journey we arrived at the crossroads. Here we set up Battalion HQ, surrounded by C Company. Quietly over the 18 set came news from B Company, then A and finally D Company, that all were at their appointed places, and everything was silent.

The roads were minor, narrow, hedged on both sides, and cobbled or sandy. The Battalion HQ carrier was actually on the crossroads, and to our right about thirty yards away was a large chateau. This had a wall, about five feet high, with iron railings on top and some recesses. It ran back from the crossroads about forty yards, and joined a very substantial barn.

Thus, at about 0430 in the stillness of the summer morning without even a bird singing, the stage was set. Quietly, one by one, the carriers stole up, and parked behind David's, which was tucked into one of the recesses in the wall. Then up came the rearguard with Jerry Weiss and my half-track. The other vehicles were parked against the wall, but as the half-track was so large it was parked against the barn with its tail sticking out into the road.

Everything was so quiet that I began to hope that a mistake had been made, and the Germans had slipped away completely. The CO reported to Brigade that all were on their objectives and there was no opposition.

The silence was broken suddenly and dramatically by a burst of Sten gun fire, about five yards from where I was standing – a sentry said that a Hun had walked up to him. Thereafter things happened rapidly. A hail of fire came from the chateau windows and all around. A Daimler scout car came up the road from the direction of B Company, but everyone held fire as we were warned that our recce were about. When it darted round to the right, followed by a VW, we knew it to be a Hun.

I was talking to Colonel Brooke when we heard the sound of tracks. I asked if they could be our tanks and he assured me that there was no possibility – in any case, they were not English tank noises. For what subsequently happened, I offer no excuse beyond circumstances which were somewhat unreal.

I was speaking to the Battery on the wireless in David's carrier. On finishing, I took off the headphones to hear the sound of tracks very close by. C Company Commander was passing and I asked him if they were our tanks – he replied that he thought they might be Churchills coming up to help. I looked down the road and saw a square turret. So thinking I must get my half-track out of the way, I ran down towards it. Suddenly, in a shower of sparks, the tank took a terrific butt at the back of my half-track, then drew back to do it again. This made me see red, as I reasoned that if he had waited a moment I would have shifted it out of the road. So I rushed up to the tank and roundly abused the chap who had his head out, then suddenly realised what I had not seen before – the long 88 mm gun and horrid coloured paint of a German Tiger tank!

Amid the confusion my hapless crew were bailing out of the half-track, and I fled back up towards Battalion HQ shouting that it was a Tiger. David and his driver grabbed the 0.5″ Browning, and I crouched behind his carrier. The tank butted my half-track clear through the wall of the stone barn, then roared up the road towards us. David fired his machine gun and I emptied my pistol at the fellow poking out of the top. The Tiger stopped on the crossroads and swung round. It hit a metal telegraph pole which crashed on to David and his driver, knocking them both a bit silly and wrecking the wireless and machine gun.

The Tiger then departed into the early morning in the direction of B Company. We all started to recover and the last chap was trying to get out of the half-track when, with a roar, two more Tigers came racing up the road. The last crewman fell out of the half-track on to the road, and the two tanks actually ran over him as he lay between the tracks! He was very frightened, but suffered only abrasions.

The CO's carrier had been driven across the road as a block. The first tank scrunched right over it – it did not seem to impede it in the least! We cautiously looked around but fortunately there were no more tanks.

After a short while there were two bangs in the direction of B Company – poor fellows, we all thought. Then came a call on the 18 set – the CO answered and a voice said, 'Sunray 2 here (OC, B Company), we had three visitors a few minutes ago. I am afraid one got away!' His company had put 75 grenades on the road and shot the second tank with a PIAT. It stopped suddenly, and the third tank ran into the back of it. All the crew bailed out and were killed or wounded.

B Company had earlier taken prisoner an awful SS major of the Hitler Jugend, who had been in the Daimler staff car. Goodness knows why we did not shoot him when he shouted for the Tigers to come to his aid. Also there was a wounded Hun on a stretcher by David's carrier, and his feelings at having a Browning fire about three inches from his face and a tank miss him by six inches are best imagined.

After this I evacuated David who was not looking well, and tried to sort out the mess. My half-track was a write-off, but I tied a wireless set together out of two. Apart from one signaller, all the rest of my crew were pretty shaken up, so I sent a request for replacements.

The CO ordered C Company to clear the chateau. As considerable fire had come from it, the NCO in charge approached the front door and fired a burst of Bren bullets through it. The door immediately swung open, and out rushed a Frenchman who threw his arms about the NCO's neck and kissed him resoundingly! He was followed by his beaming wife carrying a tray of coffee.

Battery Commander's half-track.

By 1200 things went quiet, and the Division consolidated to await the next move.

After a day or two David was as right as rain. The lad who fell under the tanks went off to hospital, but was only slightly injured and rejoined the Battery later.

After this episode came the 'Killing Ground' of the Falaise Pocket. There was much mopping up, but we played little part in these operations.

(NB. The Falaise Pocket was one of the bloodiest campaigns of the War. Despite the Allies not closing the gap ruthlessly, the fleeing Germans were attacked on all sides by Canadians, Americans, British and Poles. Over 10,000 Germans were killed, 60,000 injured, 50,000 taken prisoner, and vast resources were lost. But some 100,000 enemy escaped the net. Ed.)

CHAPTER 10
SWEEP THROUGH FRANCE
22 AUGUST TO 5 SEPTEMBER 1944

*T*wo days after the battle at Necy, my Artillery Commanding Officer, Colonel Gibson, was posted away and I was assigned to Artillery Regimental HQ as Second in Command to Major 'Chess' Chessels. It was at this time that FOO David Salmon left my Battery, and we welcomed an old friend, Captain Barnett 'Joss' Martin as his replacement.

There was very little operational role for the artillery at this time because the Huns were being rounded up from the Falaise Pocket by the Recce Regt and Armour. There was constant movement throughout the whole area and, apart from very exceptional circumstances, gun fire was not on.

One day Bob Chapman and I went on a run in the staff car to Saint-Lambert and Chambois, which were supposed to be about the worst places in the Falaise Pocket. I am sure that only the most hideous concentration camp could produce a sight or smell to compare with what was left of those two villages. There were corpses of horses lying where they had fallen in their traces – frequently the road was completely blocked by them. In places, dead Germans and unfortunate villagers lay head to foot in the gutters where they had been caught by the Typhoons. Enemy equipment, rations and stores were scattered far and wide. Worse, it was hot summer weather and the corpses were a week or more old – the stench was indescribable, as was the appearance of what were once human beings.

The Regiment was moved into action near Bierre, but we did not have to fire at all. I deployed 497 Battery pleasantly close by, and I could go across frequently to see them all.

On 23 August, Lt. Colonel F.N.W. Gore arrived to take over command of the Artillery Regiment. It was his lot to see us through all the fighting from that time to VE Day. I would like to say that we could have wished for no better command and support in battle than that which we all received from Colonel Gore. Never were orders for fire ever queried as to their necessity. No amount of trouble was too much to ensure that the forward unit was in wireless touch. By hook or by crook, the urgent call was always answered, cost what it may.

Two days later our journey across France commenced. As Major Chessels was showing the new CO around and introducing him to everyone, I continued as Artillery Second in Command. I spent most of my time ahead of the artillery regiment, planning its route. They would arrive, and off I would go on another recce. Our record was four moves in one day.

We crossed the Seine at Muids, not far from Rouen, on 29 August without any opposition.

On 2 September I rejoined 497 Battery at Doullens, and we commenced a night move forward to catch up with the Brigade recce party. On arriving at Nuncq, we found an unhappy state of affairs. The Mons had been allotted an area around a flying bomb site, which was thought to be clear. Their recce party had a fracas with enemy guards at the site, and lost one captain wounded and captured (later recaptured at Bruges) and two others seriously wounded. The 11th Hussars came to the rescue with armoured cars, but all the Huns except two had retreated by then.

Our first job was to attack and take the village of Fleurs, which was about a mile off the main road, and then the village of Conche, another half mile further on. After careful planning the attacks went in, but there was no opposition and we did not fire in either case.

Merville

Early in the morning of 5 September we arrived in a village on fairly high ground. From our vantage point in its church tower we could see the small town of Merville. Every piece of ground between ourselves and the town appeared absolutely flat with no cover at all. There was a very large airfield between us, and in the town was a high building (the Town Hall), which must have had equally good command of any move forward on our part. Intelligence reports claimed that Merville was occupied by some 800 SS troops and the airfield was supposedly mined.

At 1100 hours, Colonel Brooke received orders that The Mons were to attack and take Merville.

This was obviously an unpleasant prospect, so we started to hatch a fireplan. Then another order arrived directing that the town should not be subjected to heavy bombardment, as it was thought that the enemy might be withdrawing – cold comfort to those who were going to attack it!

We started to move gently forward. I left David Thomson in the church tower to watch our progress, and went forward with Battalion HQ. The companies moved ahead of us, and it was not long before B Company confirmed that the airfield was mined, which slowed us down.

As we were leaving the small village we were greeted by excited French as liberators, and an incident occurred which has stuck in my mind ever since. Colonel Brooke and I were standing by my half-track (I had a new one by then), when an old woman came out of a small inn with two glasses and a bottle of Calvados on a tray.

She addressed Colonel Brooke, 'Bouvez Calvados avec La France.'

The CO answered, 'Non, merci! Apres la bataille.'

The old woman, in the most sepulchral tone said, 'Bouvez maintenant, parce que vous ete pres de mort!'

It took two glasses to pull us around after that!

Then the Maquis arrived – the real Maquis. We saw many effeminate youths wearing Maquis armbands and asking for weapons, but they had enlisted when liberation was close enough to make it safe.

These two were husband and wife, small unassuming people who appeared working class. The husband was the commander of the Maquis in Merville, and his wife helped. Their role was to guide us up a covered route to get us near and unseen, then, if there was to be a

Merville after the battle.

battle, he would direct the Maquis. His wife was going off on a bicycle into Merville to warn the Maquis what time to expect us. Without any fuss she kissed her husband, shook hands with us all and rode off to go through the German lines, a highly dangerous task. I am happy to say that she made it safely, although the main bridge over the canal blew up just as she got to the far bank. I had the pleasure of seeing her the following day, safe and sound.

The companies advanced, but progress was slow as everyone was very tired. There was no shelling even though the Hun had four guns in the town square. The General came up to hurry things along, and everyone did their best to make haste. Suddenly, at about 2000 hours, a burst of Spandau fire came from the town, and then a message from B Company to say they were in. The Hun had been pulling out as the B Company patrol arrived. There was a brief battle causing some casualties, but within an hour the whole Battalion was established and Merville had fallen.

The following day was quiet, and the locals amused themselves by cutting the hair off the collaborators (or their personal enemies – it appeared to make no difference).

This shaving of heads was a hotly discussed subject, in which we took no part – watching, assisting or preventing. On the surface it was a very appropriate punishment when meted out fairly, but was disgusting and the wretched woman was a truly revolting sight on completion. It did no one any harm, save the pride and feelings of the victim. Unhappily, all too frequently we were not convinced that she was a collaborator or had a German lover, but suspected a personal grudge was being discharged.

In the evening we were ordered to move towards Bailleul. En route we were uproariously greeted by the populace, who had started a rumour that Hitler had sued for peace.

CHAPTER 11
BELGIUM
7 TO 23 SEPTEMBER 1944

*T*he regiment pulled into Bailleul in early morning drizzle, and stopped for a few hours before going on into Belgium.

We camped on the famous ridge at Passchendaele, and it was easy to see how much that bit of ground had meant to the force holding it in World War I. The following day we moved on again in the direction of Lille, but when we passed Moorslede we were told to stand fast and await orders.

The same night we commenced a forced march to Antwerp, which turned out to be terrible. There were detours because of blown bridges, and we came through Menen, Oudenarde and Alost. The route was badly signposted, and in many places where lighted signs had been erected our gallant allies had stolen the bulbs! At about 0600, I was driving the half-track when the steering locked and it ran off the road into a tree. We hit with great force and the chap next to me smashed his head into the gun ring.

We arrived in Antwerp just as our armour was liberating the city. It was truly en fete, all the girls in pretty dresses, bunting and flowers, and free drinks too – until the inhabitants discovered that their liberators had financial potential beyond their wildest dreams, and prices started to soar in a wonderful manner!

Antwerp offered many comforts and amenities that we had not enjoyed for some time, such as baths, shows and outings. There was a strange party going on along the Wilhelmina Canal. I went down to have a look one evening – it was an amazing war! One would go into the bar of a little pub, mingle with the civilians drinking there, and look at the Huns doing more or less the same thing on the other side of the canal!

Merville after the battle.

On 17 September we pushed on as a regimental column towards the River Escaut. The Mons were under the command of 158 Brigade, whose job was to force a crossing over the Escaut at Lommel. They were to protect the left flank of the troops trying to get into Germany via Nijmegen (to relieve the airborne assault at Arnhem, which of course had not commenced yet).

Opposing 158 Brigade was the German 6th Para Regiment, commanded by the famous Colonel von der Heydte. We moved with The Mons up to Lommel, and that evening were well and truly bombed by the Luftwaffe. It was most unpleasant. I lay under the half-track waiting for mine to come down, but the nearest they got was the anti-tank platoon about fifty yards away.

The following day we crossed the bridge with The Mons, moving over the frontier into Holland. I went down the bank of the canal at dusk. It was all very lonely and deserted, and after about two miles I came to a small inn and a tributary across my path. After looking around very carefully, I felt a little nervous and decided to turn back. I went back up the bank about 500 yards and was met with a sharp challenge. It was The Mons sentry who told me I had been right down to the place where they had been fighting the 6th Para that afternoon. We can only suppose that they thought I was bait for a trap and held their fire!

On 20 September, we were ordered to pull back and act as bridge guard whilst things developed. On the night of 22nd, a recce patrol went out and found itself cut off on its way back by a column of Germans moving in single file, very quietly towards the canal about 400 yards in front of our position. Later it was discovered that this was the 6th Para, who had pulled out then lost their way, so headed back to the canal. If only the patrol could have informed us – they were right in our firing zone!

On 23rd, we had orders to go down the canal bank to the inn I had visited, bridge the tributary, and advance toward Reusel on the main Eindhoven – Turnhout road. This we did without mishap, and by 0430 we were on the road which led to Postel and Reusel.

We were then ordered to push on, which led us to the battle at Voorheide.

CHAPTER 12

VOORHEIDE

24 SEPTEMBER TO 20 OCTOBER 1944

Other battalions of 158 Brigade were to secure the town of Reusel, while our orders were to guard their left flank. We were to clear the opposition, if any, from the small village of Voorheide. This was two miles west of Reusel and on the banks of a canal at right angles to the Escaut.

We made our way towards Postel at about 0730 hours, and the first problem came from mines which were liberally scattered on the road. We circumvented them after losing two carriers, and arrived in Postel, famed for its monastery. There we learned from the locals that the Hun had retreated but they did not know how far, and that the unit opposing us was the 6th Para again. Colonel von der Heydte had used the monastery as his HQ. In their opinion he was a fine soldier, and had conducted himself as a gentleman. We obviously did not share that opinion, but as Frankie Brooke said, 'When we know we are up against 6th Para, we know we have to try very hard.'

We felt our way gently forward from Postel. The column soon came in sight of the church tower at Reusel, which had caused much trouble previously to other battalions. There was no shelling this time and we turned northwards on to the canal bank. After some 500 yards we came to what was shown on the map as a dynamite factory. We were on the towpath of the canal, with trees and a bank on our right and water on our left. We did not know who was on the other bank, but we knew it was not held by us and so felt very exposed. We were warned that the towpath was mined, and about 800 yards beyond the dynamite factory lay the village of Voorheide.

D Company found some Huns in the dynamite factory and shot

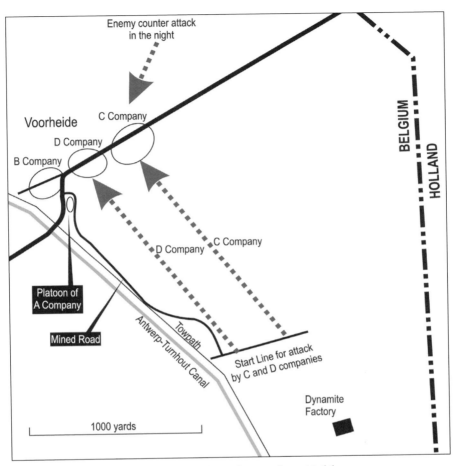

Voorheide, 24-25 September, 1944.

them up, so it was plain that there was going to be trouble in Voorheide itself. We made a fireplan using the whole regimental artillery. However shooting was a problem, as at the precise moment we started ranging the most violent jamming came over the wireless. It was only with the greatest difficulty that we got the orders through to the guns, but finally I had the fire coming down OK.

Our infantry started to move forward, and from our OP in the dynamite factory I watched their progress. I had my glasses fixed on the B Company subaltern leading a platoon up the road. Suddenly there was a flash and I saw him, or pieces of him, whirl through the air. It was

Approach to Voorheide.

horrible, and my immediate thought was that one of our guns must be firing short. A superficial check showed that to be impossible, then two more explosions occurred with more casualties and we realised that they were treading on mines.

The other companies were making good headway, and by 2000 hours C and D Companies were established in the village. B Company was still moving ahead and A Company remained with Battalion HQ, giving us protection. It was now quite dark, and the situation in the village suddenly became unpleasant. Hardly had B Company arrived when it was challenged. In the resulting spurt of fire both the officers were wounded, leaving the company under command of an NCO.

There was a very gallant display by the bearer officer and first aid men who went up and brought the wounded back from the village, in the full knowledge that there were many German paratroops around.

At 0030 Tommy Tucker, OC Pioneers, advised that the road was now cleared of all the mines they could find, so the CO decided to move A Company into the village. At 0130 the commander of A Company

Major Hughes in an OP.

returned to report that another big mine had gone off, wounding a number of his men and rendering the road impassable. It appeared that these mines were home-made from explosives in wooden boxes, and hence were not picked up by the mine detectors.

The CO then decided to remain in place until daylight, with two platoons of A Company still with us. At 0330, C Company reported a number of Huns passing by them in the village. When B Company reported the same thing, it became obvious that a serious counter attack was under way. Heavy fighting was developing all around them, so I called down defensive fire on the German line of approach.

Stragglers started arriving with alarming tales of our forward companies being overrun, and the Boche being just 150 yards from our HQ. By this time it was starting to get light and we could see what was happening. Apparently three of our platoons had tried to manoeuvre for a better position but had been driven back. B and C Companies were still holding out in their houses in the village, but between ourselves and the village were two or three hundred Boche advancing on our position.

Because we had made ready to move I had no remote control out, so had to stand by the half-track to convey fire orders. I called for radio silence, the wireless was clear, and I sent a message to every gunner that it was now or never. We must have quick and accurate response from the guns. It was not safe to use any more than one battery, so with a muttered prayer I started directing fire in between the companies and our HQ. It was pouring with rain, and the Hun was getting far too close for comfort. I gave another order to the guns, and called for fire to land about fifty yards from where I was standing. Bullets were whistling all around, and the row and smoke dulled one's senses.

As it was now getting quite light, David Thomson could see the action from his OP on top of the dynamite factory and started directing some fire. Then C Company called in some targets, and our guns really started to lay into them. The Boche now found himself in a very uncomfortable position, being shot at from all sides, and pulled out leaving sixty or seventy casualties.

However for us it had been a very close call. I must pay a very humble tribute to our gunners that September morning. But for them, this story would never have been written. I timed the response – ten seconds after the orders were passed, shells were on their way up. It was an outstanding display of artillery skill and was generously praised by the infantry.

Meanwhile the battle for Reusel had not gone well, so our position was far from comfortable. We were alone, 2,000 yards ahead of our own lines, with Hun on all sides. We spent three windy nights there.

Unreliable civilian reports claimed thousands of German reinforcements were approaching. Eventually the Brigadier decided to pull us back into our own lines until the Reusel battle was settled.

Personally, I was feeling very ill. When the counter attack was on, I had to stand in the pouring rain and got soaked. This developed into an appalling cold with a fair temperature, but I could not get away. Then Joss Martin came up, so I handed over and retired to A Echelon to try and recover. I remained there until the regiment moved up the corridor through Eindhoven toward Nijmegen.

Nijmegen Area

Whilst the battle for Voorheide was going on, aircraft and gliders carrying the airborne attack on Arnhem came over us. Of course everyone was agog to know how things were going with them, because the whole of our present role was to assist the thrust into Germany from the north. We had seen the Guards Armoured Division and the 43rd pushing northwards on our right. Scraps of information began to trickle back that the plan had not materialised, resistance was stiffer than anticipated, and that we were going to try to relieve the airborne forces at Arnhem. At the same time honour if nothing else had been satisfied, as a very small part of Germany was now occupied near Cleve, the town from whence came the celebrated Anne.

After being in Echelon for three days with Dick Potter, who was also sick, orders came to move forward. I rejoined the Battery, which was going north. As the enemy had now withdrawn from Reusel and Voorheide, the route lay through Eindhoven to Beek, where we were to harbour.

I went independently in my Jeep, and passed the area of the main advance. Vast areas were littered with gliders and crashed aircraft, the aftermath of the airborne landings.

At one point I was standing by the road. A Jeep with a chequered flag (top priority) manned by CMPs passed, followed by an open car with the Field Marshal on board. He waved in response to my salute. However more impressive to me was a staff car coming in the other direction with an ATS driver, the very first Englishwoman I had seen since leaving England in June.

The following day we moved north again near to St Odenrode, to relieve some of the American Airborne. As soon as the regiment arrived, we were ordered to move again north of Nijmegen, to relieve part of the 43rd Division who had been fighting to get to the trapped airborne troops at Arnhem. Evidence of their success was abundant as ambulances carrying the Airborne casualties streamed back down our axis. The situation was still fluid, and it was only the previous day that German armour had cut into an Royal Army Service Corps column, evidenced by a large number of their burnt out trucks.

I moved off with the recce party and reached the big bridge over the Maas at Grave, one of the great prizes of the operation. We stopped for the night, during which I began to feel ill. By the morning I was in the grip of serious gastro-enteritis. I completed my job in a semi-conscious state then awaited the arrival of the MO, who put me into a field hospital for the next three days. Large doses of sulphonamide did the trick, and I went off to Antwerp for 48 hours to complete my recovery. I returned to the Battery on Friday, 13 October, and was relieved to find nothing amiss despite a day of such ill-omen.

On 18th we were ordered to move back to a harbour area west of Grave. We had no idea what was being planned. Security for the operation that followed, together with camouflage and deception, was so good that the Hun totally misread our intentions.

On 20 October, we were briefed under strict secrecy, and the guns went to action stations near Heech. The next day, reconnaissance was carried out and final preparations made for the great battle for s'Hertogenbosch, or as it was called, 'Operation Allan'.

CHAPTER 13
THE BATTLE FOR S'HERTOGENBOSCH
22 TO 24 OCTOBER 1944

*A*ntwerp had been captured and cleared in early September, but the Germans were still holding a large portion of the ground south of the Maas and all of the Walcheren Islands which dominated the Schelde. Until the enemy were cleared from this area, Antwerp could not be used as a port as shipping could not get in or out. Unrestricted use of Antwerp was now essential to the Allies. Currently supplies were being conveyed across France and Belgium by road and rail. If we were to embark on an all-out attack on Germany, we had to have the port in operation to build up resources.

The German defences hinged upon two main towns. The most important was the communications centre of s'Hertogenbosch, and the other was Tilburg. We had bypassed them in our push towards Arnhem. Once they were taken, it would be easy to clear back to the Maas and make possible the main attack on Walcheren. As use of Antwerp was such a priority, the High Command decided to launch the whole weight of the Second Army against s'Hertogenbosch and Tilburg.

This operation was particularly significant to us, as it was the first time our 53rd Division operated as a main unit, rather than as scattered brigade and battalion support to other divisions. Accordingly the role allotted to 53rd Division was the capture of s'Hertogenbosch.

The advance would follow the railway line west for some five miles, through the villages of Geffen, Kruisstraat, Bruggen, Rosmalen, and Orthen, to reach s'Hertogenbosch. Colonel Brooke's role was right flank protection for the army, and his first objective was Kruisstraat.

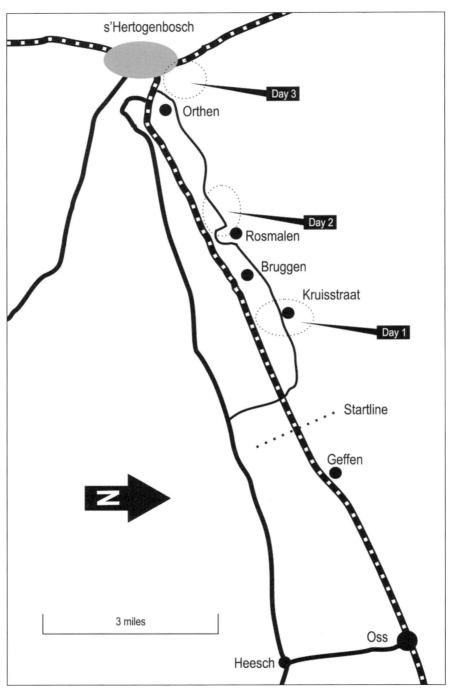

The advance to s'Hertogenbosch 22-24 October, 1944.

Captain David Thomson (2ⁿᵈ from left) prepares for action; s'Hertogenbosch.

We were to be in the village by 1400, so that the brigade destined for s'Hertogenbosch could pass through in armoured personnel carriers (Kangaroos).

The attack was to be preceded by an extensive softening up of all known gun and mortar positions by the artillery, rising to a crescendo at H Hour. For direct fire requirements I sent Joss Martin in with A Company to establish an Observation Post (OP), then David Thomson would go forward with one of the other companies as another Forward Observation Officer (FOO).

At 0545 hours, we moved out and followed the companies up to the start line. H Hour was fixed for 0630. The first flush of dawn was creeping into the sky, promising a fine day. As a result of reconnaissance, we had a very good idea of where the enemy would be likely to put down his defensive fire. When the leading company crossed the start line, down it came, just where we thought and where our troops were not! Colonel Brooke and I exchanged words of mutual congratulation.

A report came through quickly that the first objective was captured, and that the OP was established. But they could see little sign of enemy movement. Battalion HQ then moved up to the first objective. It was a terrible mess, all the houses were on fire and there were a few very dazed Huns who were obviously wondering what it was all about.

Crocodile shooting flame.

The next phase was quickly organised, and fire was arranged to support the two companies going forward. In this action we had a squadron of tanks of the Inniskilling Dragoon Guards to support the Battalion. They were good, and the infantry and tanks developed much mutual confidence as the action proceeded. The companies and tanks moved off at 0830, and for the next few hours the fighting was brisk, although at no time did we feel we were anything other than on top. Various calls for fire were coming through for opportunity targets and these were actioned speedily and effectively. About 0900 our troops were passing out of Joss' view, so I ordered David to go forward to join C Company as FOO.

The companies and tanks were making good headway, and most of my time was spent relaying calls for fire to the 4th Welch gunner who was experiencing poor wireless reception. Prisoners were coming in quickly and by midday we had accounted for an enemy battalion including its commander, a horrible little Nazi.

At 1315 we reported that we were on our objective of Kruisstraat. HQ decided to launch the thrust through us, and at 1500 the column came up but did not get very far for various reasons, particularly mines. Eventually the mounted infantry were ordered to dismount, and the E. Lancs told to develop a new approach during the hours of darkness.

Orders came for our Battalion to go forward at dawn, supported by the tanks and Crocodiles, clear the village of Bruggen and secure

Rosmalen. Our plan was for A Company to lead the attack, and D and B Companies to cover left and right respectively. Artillery support would be provided from every available gun within range, which numbered some hundreds.

This battle was brief. We blasted everything with gunfire. Then A Company went in hell for leather with the tanks and Crocodiles, and they blasted every living thing. At first they were troubled by some Boche in trenches along the side of the road which was on a dyke. But as soon as the Crocodiles rolled their flame down the bank the Huns packed it in. Those that were caught died horribly, or if they were not so lucky were just burnt. The screams of the German wounded took a lot of the fight out of the rest.

Again we caught a whole German battalion. They had been sent there from Tilburg the previous night, and were to await an inevitable British attack that would come in great strength. The commander said he had intended to fight, but had lost 150 men in the first twenty minutes so decided to surrender.

Our push was delayed a little by some Self Propelled 88 mm guns that were moving around and engaging our tanks and infantry. Although I had both OPs out, we could not shoot freely because of the close country and the fact that our troops were surging forward and not always visible.

At about 1530 we were in the outskirts of Rosmalen. I got a report from the tanks that they were being shelled and had seen a gun flash about 1,000 yards in front. I was computing this when D Company called in almost the same map reference. This appeared to be a significant threat, so I called for an 'Uncle Target' (the entire Divisional Artillery of 72 guns), Scale 5. As the guns reported they were ready, B Company also called to say they were held up by shelling. I ordered fire. A lyrical voice from the tanks reported a hit, so I ordered a repeat fire, Scale 10. I was told of a large number of Germans running in all directions, so I called for fire by the entire Corps Artillery ('Yoke Target', about 200 guns), Scale 10. This made the ground in the area positively rise up and no more shells came back.

Colonel Brooke (left) with a lieutenant.

Half an hour after this incident we reported that we were on our objective of Rosmalen, and we dug in for the night. On our left the 6th Royal Welsh Fusiliers went through towards Hintham to cut off any Huns trying to slip back into s'Hertogenbosch during the night. They were very successful as many were doing just that. We had an incident or two during the night with wandering SP guns, but the RWF advance was very successful.

The Mons were ordered to send a patrol out along the dyke and try to get to Orthen, which task they accomplished successfully. The rest of the Battalion moved through my big target, and we established our HQ in a round fort that gave one great confidence when the shells came down.

The area of the previous days artillery target contained a complete German battery knocked out, every gun smashed, every vehicle a wreck, and every horse dead. The slit trenches were full of dead Huns, and there were bits of dead everywhere. It was without doubt the most complete kill I ever had.

The Battalion then went into a holding phase at Orthen, while others went through to clear s'Hertogenbosch and Tilburg. S'Hertogenbosch was finally captured by 158 Brigade on 24 October.*

*Excerpt from The History of the 2nd Battalion The Monmouthshire Regiment:

'The spirited action by the 2nd Monmouths contributed in no small degree to the capture on the following day of s'Hertogenbosch by the 158 Brigade and was recognised by the award of the D.S.O. to Lt. Col. Brooke, who was also personally congratulated on the Battalion's achievements by both the Army and the Corps Commanders when he met them in the town while the fighting on the 24th was still going on. In its advance of nearly 7,000 yards in the two days, the 2nd Monmouths had destroyed two German battalions, a result largely ascribable to the unfailing support of tanks and 'Crocodiles', and the extremely quick and accurate shooting of 133rd Field Regiment, R.A. (Panteg), and in particular of 497 Battery, whose shells were often in the air within one minute of a call for fire. It was in fact a triumph of teamwork, with every man engaged doing his full share with skill, courage and endurance.'

Military Cross
By the Editor

In recognition of his conduct and contribution to the battle to liberate s'Hertogenbosch, Major Hughes was awarded the Military Cross.

The MC is granted for 'exemplary gallantry in the face of the enemy'. It is the third highest award for valour conferred by the British Army, ranking behind only the VC (Victoria Cross) and DSO (Distinguished Service Order).

The citation accompanying the letter from King George VI reads as follows:

'The Military Cross
Major (temporary) Richard Hughes, (56398)
Royal Regiment of Artillery

Major HUGHES is Battery Commander of 497 Field Battery which is affiliated to 2ⁿᵈ Battalion Monmouthshire Regiment.

During the operations 22ⁿᵈ/25ᵗʰ October, 1944, culminating in the capture of s'HERTOGENBOSCH, 2ⁿᵈ Battalion Monmouthshire Regiment advanced on a narrow front along the only road available on the exposed right flank. Throughout the four days Major HUGHES was continually up and down this axis reconnoitring Observation Posts and organising fire support to enable the advance to continue, showing complete disregard for his own safety and a determination to provide the maximum artillery support at all costs. By his energy and vigilance he managed, when communications were bad, to get fire orders back to the guns not only of his own battery but to those of other Observation Posts supporting the forward battalions, thereby largely contributing to the success of the artillery support as a whole.

But for his outstanding courage and devotion to duty during these critical days, the advance on the right flank would not only have cost many more casualties to our own tanks and infantry but might also have been considerably delayed.

Major HUGHES efforts are an example of how determination and leadership can influence the provision of artillery support, have been an example to his own battery and have further added to the already considerable confidence which the infantry had in their artillery.'

CHAPTER 14

ASSAULT CROSSING OF THE WESSEM CANAL

14 NOVEMBER 1944

After moving down from s'Hertogenbosch we were ordered into action between Kinroy and Weert. We were to be prepared to support the infantry in the event of a counter attack. As the whole Second Army had been concentrated on the attack to free Antwerp, this sector had only been held by the Belgian Brigade. Intelligence suggested that the Germans understood this weakness, and were to launch an attack to the south west through this sector.

We were to recce the area to be able to cope with an attack, then work out a plan to force a crossing over the Wessem Canal and drive the Hun back over the Maas. A large force was involved, including 51st Highland and 53rd Welsh Divisions. This was known as Operation Bristol.

Our assault would be made by The Mons and 4th Welch, with 6th Royal Welsh Fusiliers going through to secure the bridgehead. The operation would be supported by about 400 guns, plus tanks and Crocodiles. The guns would initially soften up the enemy strong points, the tanks and Crocodiles would go on to the canal bank and shoot flame and bullets on to the opposite bank, while the infantry would go down to the river with assault boats and cross to the other side.

The plan for The Mons was for B and C Companies to cross the canal on the right and left respectively, D Company would follow, and A Company would secure the near bank. Battalion HQ, including myself, would cross with our wireless sets and carriers on Buffaloes (large amphibious tracked vehicles). Joss would go over with the first companies, and David would remain on our side of the canal, controlling the wireless battle when I crossed over. He would also be in a position to organise close defence, if the whole operation went sour and we were forced back over the canal. I decided as a final precaution to have a spare wireless set mounted in a handcart and brought down to Battalion HQ.

So the final plans were laid, and all we had to do was clean our weapons, check on everything, and wait for H Hour which was 2000 hours.

During the day we heard that 51st Highland had made their crossing and were going ahead without too much opposition, so we hoped our job was not going to be too hard.

At 1900 the companies started to move off. Joss went with them, and the guns started their opening salvos. We made ready to get into Battalion HQ on our side of the river at H Hour. The choice of this exposed site had filled Colonel Brooke and me with a great deal of foreboding, but there was nowhere else to put it, so shells or no shells, there we had to be.

Promptly at 2000 the artillery barrage lifted from the canal line, and dozens of searchlights were switched on to give light for the operation. Then followed the glare of the Crocodiles as they projected their flame across the water. It was a most dramatic moment.

We set up Battalion HQ in the arranged position, and immediately discovered our foreboding was justified as the first salvo of shells arrived. We hastily parked our vehicles and got our gunner command post dug into a ditch with a bit of head cover, just as the next salvo arrived. There were two Buffaloes parked in our midst for the purpose of carrying the CO and myself. This salvo hit one and set it on fire, killing most of the crew. It did nothing for our peace of mind to be told that it was also carrying 200 lbs of high explosive, in addition to its normal ammunition which was going off like a series of firecrackers. However it was hopeless to try to move, so all we could do was hope that the explosive was damp or that it would turn out to be face powder or something.

The companies were making their way across the canal. We heard over the air that C Company was over OK, but that B Company on the right had put a platoon over which had walked straight into a minefield. They were heavily engaged by Spandau and other small arms fire, with the result that all but two of the platoon were wiped out.

It was obvious that no more troops could be sent over at that point, as the approach was a bottleneck through a minefield and they could only get one boat down at a time. The CO then decided to send D Company over at the left hand crossing, with orders to clear down to the right. This they did but it took some two hours in rearrangement, and it created a problem because a bridge was supposed to be built over the canal at the right hand crossing.

Around 0230 Colonel Brooke, who was very unwell with a bad cold, decided to move Battalion HQ over the canal. At regular intervals of fifteen minutes shells had dropped on us, so we had to time our departure to miss them. As the Buffaloes were out of action, we had to resort to the unwieldy perambulators and handcarts to move our gear. I left David sitting in the hole in the ground and in touch with Joss, who was still with D Company.

Taking two signallers, I trundled off down the track to the boat. Lugging and heaving a very heavy perambulator through the mud, up one bank, down the other and on to the exposed mud, was neither pleasant nor easy. We sweated and scrambled and hung on. Somehow we got into a boat and paddled our way across. The canal was not too wide, with very little current. The night sky was illuminated by many searchlights and the glare of burning houses. Shells were landing in the canal, and every so often a short round aimed at Battalion HQ would drop into the water close by. However we got ashore and manhandled everything into a farm building on the bank which was not too badly damaged. It was getting bitterly cold and an icy wind was blowing through the farmhouse.

By now resistance seemed to be weakening, and the companies got on to the final bridgehead line just as day was breaking. After arranging defensive fire, there was nothing further to do until the bridge was built. I began to feel very hungry. As the shelling was only going on over the proposed bridge site, I wandered back on to the bank to see what was happening, and whether there was any sign of new Buffaloes with our carriers. The vehicles with breakfast appeared on the far bank, so we scrambled back and had a very good meal. I then wandered back on to the bank to wait for the carriers.

It was then I saw a dreadful sight, and had cause to thank the divine power that had guided my footsteps that far. As I was watching a Buffalo come across, a man walked down the bank where our party had been the previous night and where I had walked just half an hour ago. There was a bang, and he collapsed with his foot blown off, having stood on a Schumine. Somebody ran to help him, there was another bang, and the same thing happened. I was quite helpless standing on the opposite bank, but a party arrived and, with due caution, rescued these two and sent them off to hospital. The pioneers went off to get some tape and minefield signs. While the place was left, two more men ran over the bank, and before anyone could stop them they ran down the same path that we had all been using. With sickening reports two mines went up, killing one and wounding the other. Even today I go cold when I remember the way that we were all scrambling down the bank in the dark, and in some way missed every mine. Nearly two thousand mines were subsequently lifted from that area alone.

All this time Colonel Brooke had been in the farm feeling worse and worse. We sent for the MO, and he persuaded the Colonel to go back to the field hospital in Weert to recover. Major Tyler took over. We remained in place while the bridge was completed, then other brigades came through and we had a very sound sleep.

The next afternoon we were ordered to push on to the village of Beegden on the Maas. We moved out as a column at dusk, and after encountering no life at all we came to the dark village, which was rather creepy. We did find a civilian who said that the Germans had pulled out. Based on this information, we cautiously occupied the whole place and arranged defensive fire as necessary. Then came reports that the companies were all on their objectives, and we realised that Operation Bristol was complete – namely that the Hun had been forced back clear over the River Maas for its whole length.

After this followed a period of moving up and down, garrisoning the various sectors of the river. While so employed we heard first that Major Alf Chaston had been awarded the MC for his leadership and courage at Voorheide. Then two days later came the news that Colonel Brooke had been awarded the DSO for his command of the Battalion at s'Hertogenbosch, and Brigadier Coleman also got the DSO for his part in the same battle. All were truly well earned decorations.

CHAPTER 15
ON THE MAAS
NOVEMBER/DECEMBER 1944

*F*ollowing the crossing of the Wessem Canal, our role throughout the remainder of the year was to occupy the west bank of the River Maas, harass the enemy where possible, and defend against any counter attack. There was also to be some rest and recuperation and leave during December.

The village of Beegden had very little damage, and a comfortable Battalion HQ was set up there. My Battery was nearby in Baexam, and well accommodated although the farms were a bit squalid and smelly. The guns looked their normal fresh, pristine selves, and as it seemed no major battle was imminent there was a feeling of wellbeing.

We were facing the Hun across a wide stretch of the Maas, and had a fairly unrestricted view of his activities as he dug in on the other side. Our ammunition was rationed to about four rounds per gun per day except in an emergency, so very little shooting took place. Interestingly, the amount of shelling we could do with this quota was just enough to produce retaliation (as I found out the first day), but quite insufficient to stop the enemy counter fire. A policy of 'live and let live' therefore existed between us.

One exception was on 17 November, when the whole regiment fired 72 rounds at our first target in Germany – we then began to feel we were striking at the very lair of the beast itself!

We made one or two moves up and down the river, and were generally on the alert for enemy patrols. Indeed, one night at a narrower part of the Maas, a sudden skirmish occurred around A Company when a German patrol stumbled upon their sentry.

A rest area had been organised for our artillery regiment near Weert,

Major Hughes reading a map.

and one battery would be taken out at a time. The turn of 497 Battery came on 9 December, and we went back for five days. It was wonderful to experience many of the amenities of civilised life, like a comfortable bed, a bath, a change of clothes, electric light, wireless, and so on. Well rested, we returned to action stations at Baexam on 14 December.

On 18 December orders came that we were to be relieved, and that we should move to an area north of Brussels for a rest and Christmas.

This was the first occasion that the entire Division would be out of action since the landings, and everyone was ready to relax. After an uneventful journey, the Battery settled into a delightful little village called Pippelherde – completely undamaged, clean and bright, with ample accommodation.

The next morning I received orders to go on 48 hours leave to Brussels. I was not keen on this but there was no arguing, so I set off, telling my driver to return on 21st. By chance I ran into Colonel Brooke and Jerry Weiss, and we had a jolly evening.

There had been some rumours about a German counter attack. The following morning staff cars with flags waited outside the hotel, dispatch riders came and went, and leave was obviously being cancelled. Our Battalion was to move south at once to the River Dyle, between Brussels and Louvain.

What had happened gradually became clear. The Huns under Field Marshal von Rundstedt had attacked the Americans through the Ardennes with great speed and energy. Their intention was to get to Antwerp, and from the speed of their initial breakthrough they would be upon us by nightfall. The 'Battle of the Bulge' had commenced.

Our job was to hold the line of the Dyle no matter what happened.

Having made his move to stir up ordinary mortals, the Almighty then pulled the plug and down came the snow and a biting wind.

The Mons set up their Battalion HQ in a village main square, which was very comfortable. I had a room and command post in a house next door, and the three old women who owned it kept a wonderful fire going throughout.

After two days the Germans did not seem to be making much headway, so we decided to spend Christmas where we were. We had several parties which were a great success.

The Ardennes

On 29 December we were warned to expect a move to the south. I went with Colonel Brooke to meet the Brigadier near Namur for orders. We sped through snow covered countryside. Along the roadside were piled aircraft bombs and ammunition, all of which would have been lost had the enemy broken through. The country seemed to become more forbidding as we approached Namur – which, with Liege, were the two fortress cities of Belgium, and were the first to be ravaged in World War I. I found Namur to be a grim place, dark and grey, as if conscious of the role it had played throughout history as one of the buffers of Europe.

We crossed the Meuse and went on towards the rendezvous at Ciney. We saw the first signs of the German thrust, with some burnt out cars and light armoured vehicles. From there the road became strewn with smashed enemy transport. I began to get a feeling of admiration for the Americans, who obviously had thrown themselves at the Hun wherever he had appeared, and by sheer bitter determination and with tremendous losses had hurled him back.

Our orders were to relieve the Americans near Rochefort, to allow them to regroup. Having looked over the ground we returned to Louvain, and the following day the Division started streaming down the road to Namur and the Ardennes. Many were the friendly waves and smiles as we passed through Namur, and the people seemed pleased and relieved to see us.

It was bitterly cold and there were blocks of ice floating on the Meuse. The sky promised more snow. We passed through Ciney towards our destination. Everywhere were signs of battle. It was evident how confident the Hun had been of a clear breakthrough by the number of vehicles we saw lying wrecked and burnt by the roadside. It was snowing heavily, and a bitter wind cut through all clothing.

Our Battalion assembled in the badly damaged village of Boissonville, three miles northwest of Rochefort. We were to relieve the Americans who had halted the advance in our sector, and who were now forming up for a heavy attack to drive back 'the Bulge'.

The villagers had been badly frightened. They told us that the troops who had attacked them were SS, led and commanded by a woman. This was the first time I had heard of a German woman taking part in field operations. Subsequently a woman acting as gunner was found dead in a tank in the area.

After the American battalion had moved off, the CO and I visited the companies and had a look around the area. The snow had eased a little and a wintry sun shone through. The view from the village towards the enemy positions brought on a wave of nostalgia – the rolling country resembled almost exactly the South Downs, a complete replica of the last hills before Folkestone.

Once more we were impressed by the magnificence of the American effort. In the area around our village were a total of sixteen Tiger tanks destroyed. These had attempted to bypass the American tanks in Boissonville, but in turn the Americans had outflanked the Tigers. Anyone familiar with tank warfare appreciates the difficulties involved in killing Tigers with Sherman tanks which had only 75 mm cannon. This weapon could penetrate a Tiger at only very few points. To outmanoeuvre and knock out Tigers on this scale was an achievement of guts and bravery which will seldom have been equalled.

So ended the Old Year, as this was 31 December, 1944.

CHAPTER 16
THE ARDENNES
JANUARY 1945

On New Years Day 1945, Colonel Brooke and I went to visit the 4th Welch in Rochefort for two reasons. One was that some French officers were being passed through the German lines – to do what, nobody knew. Everyone thought they were taking a huge risk and doubted that they would get away with it. Evidently the Hun agreed – when a patrol later searched the now deserted village opposite, they found the Frenchmen all neatly tied up, cold and hungry but otherwise unharmed!

The other reason was to have a drink with Major Burnett, their Second in Command, who was about to depart on leave to England – the very first person in our Brigade to do so.

On returning to Battalion HQ in Boissonville, I walked across to see the Battery who were only a few hundred yards away and existing in intense discomfort. They were in the open with only a small wood for cover, and it was nigh impossible to dig gunpits and command posts as the ground was frozen to the hardness of rock.

After various orders and counter-orders, we were told to relieve the Americans at Hotton. We had to bivouac the night in a wood, and suffered heavy snow and a severe frost. My crew were lucky as Battalion HQ had found a tiny house and we had one room.

On 3 January we took over from the Americans in a holding role, with all our troops in the village of Hotton itself except for one Company which was dug into the slopes outside.

The main road through Hotton leads southwest to Rochefort. The countryside is mountainous with sharp slopes and sheer sided valleys, and is over 1,000 ft above sea level. The River Ourthe flows through

Hotton towards Bastogne – at that time it was wide and fast flowing, with great chunks of ice swirling down it.

On the left of the river, the American 1st Army was preparing to attack in great strength to cut off the German 'bulge'. The British forces were to advance on the right, and our job was to move along the river itself.

Thus the scene was set, and on 5 January the Americans launched their great attack. This was very successful, a lot of headway was made, but they were getting their right flank shot up by the Huns on our British side of the river.

At 1830 hours orders came through that The Mons were to be placed under command of 158 Brigade, and the whole Brigade would attack the following morning to protect the American right flank.

On return from the 'O' Group, I had to commence hurried planning. I had only Joss Martin with me as Forward Observation Officer, other battery officers having been seconded elsewhere. I decided to take Peter Drane up as the other FOO. I also had to organise batteries, petrol, code signs, maps, rations and the hundred and one other things that are required in a battle.

The battle plan for The Mons was to advance from Hotton. We should secure the high ground on the right of the river, and simultaneously advance along the lower road beside the river to take the village of Rendeux Bas. This sounded quite simple in view of the fact that there was very considerable artillery and tank support. C Company (Major Alf Chaston) and D Company (Captain Phillips) would go over the top to command our objective from above. B Company (Major Jourdain) would advance along the road by the river, occupy a strategically important mill, then push on into Rendeux Bas itself. A Company would be held in reserve. I ordered Joss to go with C Company as FOO, and held Peter Drane in reserve.

The Brigade moved out at first light, and The Mons proceeded up from Hotton on to the snow covered hillside to await our order to attack.

The first problem was getting the tanks to grip on the ice covered paths and rocks. Those with rubber tracks had some purchase and did make it, but those with steel tracks were unable to climb the gradients.

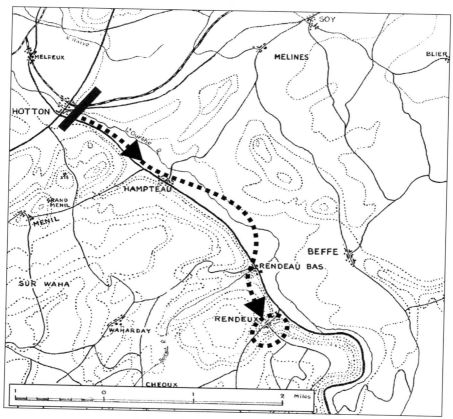

Part of the Ardennes, 2 to 8 January, 1945.

A few shells came back at us, then the snow started again. As far as we could make out, other battalions were getting ahead but not having it all their own way. One issue was mines – unusually unpleasant, as they were covered in snow and therefore invisible.

At 1130 hours, Brigade ordered The Mons to start. I laid on a small fireplan. Then came trouble – Joss found his carrier was absolutely incapable of getting up the hill as its tracks spun on the ice. So he took a signaller and a 38 set, and pushed off on foot with C Company.

The first report we received was that the tanks were having great difficulty in getting through the frozen scrub and were not keeping up with the infantry. Then came a report that C and D Companies were held up. They had come to the edge of the wood fringing the track from

Rendeux Bas to Cheoux, and found they were on one side of a cutting with almost sheer sides. On the opposite side, well dug in, was a Panther tank which was able to cover the entire road, and Spandaus covered every possible line of approach. Various flanking moves were tried, but all were frustrated and the situation was deadlocked. We waited to hear from B Company on the lower road.

B Company had set off with a troop of tanks down the road, which soon narrowed with a steep cliff on the right. So Major Jourdain put a platoon on top of the cliff, and one carried on down the road with the tanks. The platoon on the cliff ran into the same gorge as had C and D Companies, and was likewise stopped.

The platoon on the road moved forward without opposition, but found that there was a bend at the mill and the road had been blocked by several felled trees. This site was well covered by anti-tank guns and protected by mines on the riverside. The tanks were compelled to stop. But as all seemed quiet and nothing moved, the leading section made its way through the roadblock and into the mill. The Hun then reacted with great violence, forcing our troops out of the mill and into the river where some froze to death. The section commander remained with two men in the mill pool, fighting with rifles and Bren guns for some nine hours, despite all three having been wounded in the initial assault. One subsequently died.

With the enemy completely alert and firing at every movement, the situation was a deadlock. We received details of the enemy locations, so Colonel Brooke and I tried to come up with a fireplan. However when I worked out the angle of descent for the shells, I found that I could not hit the enemy positions because they were too far down into the ravine.

All this time we had been standing on a hillside in a blizzard. As dusk fell, a recce party was sent to try to find somewhere for Battalion HQ for the night, where we could use some light. A little house was found in Hampteau and we moved down.

The whole Battalion was still deployed on and around the hillside. Company commanders, including Joss, were called in to Battalion HQ. Our orders were to continue the attack through the night. What we really needed was support from the American guns, who could fire at the Huns from across the river. My CO, Colonel Gore, went to arrange this, and returned to say that the Yanks were very willing to help, and that after daylight we could have as much artillery as was available. I sent Joss over to them as FOO.

Colonel Brooke and I talked things over, and hoped our recommendation to wait for daylight would be accepted. The more I investigated the question of shooting, the more worried I became about hitting the crest on which our own troops were deployed. So we hoped against hope that we should be allowed to wait for the Americans at daybreak.

However, at 2300 one of those orders arrived which seemed to show so little understanding but was, I suppose, necessary. Briefly it stated that the General orders The Mons to attack by night and to be on their objective by morning. Then a further message to our CO: the General directs that maximum Sheldrake (artillery) be used.

It was very unusual for orders issued by the General to be sent directly to a battalion, so we thought we had better do something about it. I prepared a fireplan, codenamed 'April', which called for support from all available field regiments. It would last for about 20 minutes, during which some 5,820 shells would be fired.

Colonel Brooke decided that he would pull the Battalion back out of contact and feed them. Everyone should try to get some rest, then we would attack at 0600. He reasoned that if we were going to succeed we should do so between 0600 and daybreak, but if we could not get ahead then daylight would be better in order to see where we were.

I thought it would be good to try 'April', and put the suggestion to Colonel Brooke. He agreed, so about 0100 I ordered 'April Fire'. It was an impressive display, and to my relief most of the fire went over the vital crest.

At 0530, prior to the attack, I repeated 'April'. By this time the companies had moved up. Unfortunately, this time a proportion of the shells fell short. The temperature had fallen dramatically over the previous few hours, causing the reduction in range of our fire. Tragically,

Freezing conditions in the Ardennes.

without doing the enemy a great deal of harm, some of the medium shells fell among B Company on the crest, with some casualties.

The day wore on. We moved to an advanced Battalion HQ, but no further progress was made. No tanks could get over the ice. No guns could reach the Huns. Joss, on the other side of the river with the Yanks, could see our plight but could not engage the enemy. The situation was at an impasse – but worse, in a temperature well below zero everyone was beginning to suffer from exposure.

Eventually orders came that The Mons were to be relieved by the Recce Regt the following day. In due course the relief was effected, and The Mons, very tired, very battle weary, and very cold, pulled back into Hotton.

I was detailed to remain and provide gunnery support to the Recce Regt. This was a pleasure, as they were a delightful crowd whom I knew well. Their role was only a holding one which involved minimal stress.

The next day urgent orders came for me to rejoin The Mons who were once more going into action. This was 10 January and, except for one night, all had been exposed to the fierce weather for five days continuously. I went as quickly as possible, to find that the 5th Welch had had a very bad time at Menil, and that The Mons were relieving them. At Battalion HQ I was told that Colonel Brooke was forward with one of the companies, so I followed him up. Through frozen woods, ice covered tracks and hillsides, the ice had transformed into glaciers. If possible, the weather seemed even colder.

We were in close contact with the Hun – some 50 yards apart in places. Having done my own recce and placed Peter Drane as FOO with Alf Chaston in C Company, I went back to Battalion HQ and took over responsibility for artillery support from my opposite number.

All that remained was to hold, as we had no other orders. At about 0200 on 12 January there was a rumour that the Hun was pulling back, so we were ordered to advance. C Company went ahead to the village in front of them and when daylight came it was clear that the Hun was retreating.

The Great Attack was failing!!! Fought gallantly by the American army at the critical point in the 'bulge', and subsequently pressured by the British, the position for the Hun was becoming untenable.

We kept edging forwards. In the evening came the welcome news that we were to be relieved by the 51st Highland Division the following day. This was effected about 2230 on 13th and we left the Scotsmen in charge of our little bit of Ardennes. We went back to Hotton, ready to move out the following day.

We moved to Liege on 14 January. There I stayed in a farmhouse with delightful people and a charming daughter, for whom I fell completely – she was six, and full of fun! (Monsieur, voulez vous jouer avec moi?)

On 21 January we moved to Hellmond in Holland and settled there for a few days. Then I went on leave to England on 25th, and, of course, had a wonderful time!

The MC was awarded to Major Jourdain who, despite being wounded early in the action, continued to lead B Company with skill and determination throughout the fight. Cpl. Hutton, the Section Commander at the mill, was awarded the DCM for his outstanding act of bravery.

I shall never forget the Ardennes. Apart from the terrible weather and conditions, this was the only occasion in the entire campaign that The Mons failed to gain their objective. Even from this, they emerged 'bloody but unbowed'.

CHAPTER 17

'OPERATION VERITABLE' REICHSWALD FOREST; WEEZE

FEBRUARY 1945

*T*he Reichswald Forest

The massive counter attack by the Germans had delayed the Allied advance across Europe by a month. Now that the Battle of the Bulge had been won, the next objective for Allied Command was to clear the enemy from the land between the two great rivers, and drive him back over the Rhine into Germany. This was to be known as 'Operation Veritable'.

I returned from leave in England, arriving on the morning of 6 February at Bourg-Leopold where there were whispers of a 'big operation' being organised. There was, as yet, no indication of what it was. I met one of the officers from 331 Field Regiment who was going on leave, and he told me that the Division was stationed in and around Nijmegen.

I found a three quarter ton truck from the Regiment which was free to go. Although the driver had no map nor map coordinates, he assured me he knew just where our Regiment was, so at 1530 we set off. After some wrong turns we arrived in Nijmegen, whereupon he ran through the town, assuring me the Regiment was billeted in a school. I asked the name but he did not know. It was now pitch dark and raining. We stopped and asked an M.P. He did not know where the Regiment was, but indicated a doubtful looking track which he said ended up in Groesbeek. At this the driver announced joyfully that we were alright, and he proceeded to drive straight through Groesbeek, on towards the Reichswald Forest and into the German defences. Fortunately for us our

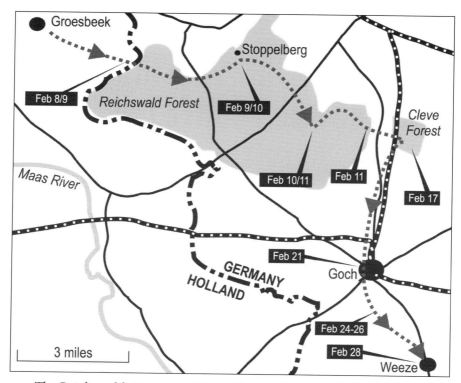

The Reichswald; Operation Veritable, 8 February – 7 March, 1945.

forward line was occupied by a Canadian patrol, who were not pleased to see a truck with all its lights on – and made it abundantly clear what they thought!

To cut a long story short, we did find the Regiment – right in the middle of Nijmegen! There I first heard the name 'Operation Veritable', and learned that it was then 'D minus 2'. 'D Day' was 8 February. The Canadian, British, and American Armies were to launch simultaneous attacks in concert.

The role of our 53rd (Welsh) Division was to advance through Groesbeek and down into the Reichswald Forest (already explored by me!), clearing it as they went and breaching the Siegfried defences en route.

We were part of 160 Brigade, which included 6th Royal Welsh Fusiliers and 4th Welch Regiments, and The Mons (advancing in that order, then

Entry to the Reichswald Forest.

leapfrogging one another). Each had a squadron of Churchill tanks and a troop of M10s (self-propelled 105 mm guns) in support. There was an enormous number of guns available, and all divisions had been moved up secretly with identification marks painted out.

D Day came and we moved to our forming up area, which was behind a belt of woods some distance back from the enemy lines. The artillery zone was on a slight rise in the ground. From where I was standing one commanded a large arc, and a faint mist hung at low level. As the opening barrage commenced, I came to appreciate the immense weight of firepower being forced upon the Hun – it seemed that from every square yard, a pencil of flame sprang out and the arc reverberated to the concussion of gunfire. With a vengeance, the British Army 'was going in!'

We remained there for some hours, then it was our turn to move up. Through villages reduced to shattered rubble and with the night lit up by the glare of burning buildings, we gradually moved forward. As a result of shelling and the tanks, the road was a rutted track which the rain had turned into a morass. It was impossible to move off the

Entry to the Reichswald Forest.

road otherwise the vehicle would sink. This did in fact happen to Joss' armoured OP, so he left it and joined me in my half-track. (As a matter of interest, his carrier went down on that first night. Traffic was so heavy on the road that it was a week before anyone could stop to pull it out.)

Dawn was not far off when we crossed the frontier into Germany, and into the Reichswald Forest. Soon we passed through 6 RWF, who had dug into ground defences. For an unhappy half hour on the edge of the woods we were exposed to fire from several gun positions, which were eventually neutralised by our M10s. We then passed through the 4th Welch, and reached our first bound.

Life in that forest destroyed any romantic illusions one might have had about Robin Hood – wet, cold, and miserable, we waited for news. The first that I had was bad. Dick Potter, a most valued Gun Position Officer, had stood on a Schumine and had his foot blown off.

After about 12 hours, the 4th Welch moved forward a bit and we followed them. The Hun celebrated the occasion by giving us an awful time. We had just pulled into a park beside the one road through the wood, when he let us have it. My Jeep driver was slightly wounded, and of course the water cans turned into colanders. This rather one-sided performance continued for some time.

Captain Joss Martin – happy, as usual!

We were more or less forced to use the existing tracks through the woods, and these had turned into quagmires. The Hun moved around outside the forest with SP guns and tanks, and fired on us whenever he thought fit – which was very frequently!

Darkness was approaching. Our Churchill tanks, magnificent things, were out of ammunition and had to come in. We settled down to get an hour or two's sleep – fully dressed, on wet ground, with every so often a nearby crump.

Colonel Brooke in Battalion HQ dugout.

About 0500 hours we got under way again. As we started forward, the leading companies were given a dreadful beating. It was intensely unpleasant. Then the popular tank squadron commander was blasted in the head and face when a mortar hit his tank – he died soon afterwards. However we pushed ahead, with the enemy falling back but beating up our lines of approach.

We were going ahead slowly through thick mud when the chain on one of my tracks came off, and got caught up. This was serious – I had only one FOO and he was ahead, so without me Battalion HQ had no gunnery officer. We frantically cut and tore at the refractory chain, all the while keeping an ear cocked for the sound of the next flock of shells. Just as I was getting really desperate, a burst of shells hit all around us, the half-track gave a lurch, and the chain dropped off – problem solved!

Our companies were getting near the far edge of the forest by this time, and Battalion HQ was established in a farm house. One company with Churchills and an FOO moved down to the edge, and they had a weird experience when some disoriented Germans joined their column in the forest.

Major Hughes in Reichswald Forest.

On 16 February, Joss's mired carrier was finally recovered and brought up. On this day, E Troop of 497 Battery fired the 1,000,000th shell of the campaign from the Divisional Artillery.

During previous days, from the edge of the Reichswald we could clearly see the Forest of Cleve. Every hour of every day it was Typhooned, shelled, or mattressed (rocketed), as it was known to be occupied by

Captain Grey in dugout near Weeze.

Huns and tanks. By 16 February, there were indications that these forces were trying to get out, so we were ordered to attack and clear it the following day. A very heavy fireplan was prepared on call, but we moved forward and achieved our objective without opposition. Except for about five bomb-happy prisoners, there were only corpses and wrecked equipment to witness our arrival.

By this time our transport and equipment situation was very poor. All the carriers and wheeled vehicles were in bad shape because of the mud. My half-track needed a lot of new equipment after having much shot away. Our supplies were then totally dependent on the amphibious Weasels – magnificent vehicles. So at 1200 hours on 18 February, we were put at six hours notice so that cleaning and maintenance could be done.

I had another urgent problem. David Thomson was going on leave and I had only one Captain. I heard that an old friend, Dennis Bishop, was at the RHU (Reinforcement Holding Unit) – probably in Bourg-Leopold – so I decided to see if I could find him. After a wild ride I did so, and the RHU were most obliging and released him immediately.

Casualty passing a 'flail' tank.

After getting Dennis' kit, we went to Louvain for the night, then early the following morning turned back towards the battle front.

On my return I found that the 'rest' had been cancelled. The Mons had moved forward to Goch, and were preparing for what developed into the bloodiest of all our battles.

Goch; Weeze; The Battle for '2 Mons Wood'

The next important objective on our axis was the little town of Weeze. It was on the main road south of Goch, and was situated in the loop of a river. A tributary cut the main road and also a minor road leading into the town. Between Goch and Weeze was a small belt of woods (to become known as '2 Mons Wood').

When I arrived a truly horrifying plan was being created. Fortunately it was abandoned later, but is worth recounting.

We knew that the main bridge into town was blown, but there was a very minor road through the woods leading into Weeze. It was hoped that the bridge on this road was still intact. The plan was for one company,

Knocked out German gun.

with tanks, to secure the woods, then the rest of the Battalion would rush through in Kangaroos (armoured troop carriers) to secure the bridge into Weeze. It was assumed that the belt of woods was not occupied.

24 hours before this original plan was due to take place air recce showed a fair amount of enemy strength in the woods, so the plan was changed. The new plan was for the entire Mons Battalion with a squadron of tanks (13/18 Hussars) to attack and secure the belt of woods.

As an operation it was fairly straightforward. All four companies were to be committed, one right, one left, one central, and one in reserve in the rear. Battalion HQ would be based in the southernmost building in Goch, then follow the companies down as they progressed. Dennis Bishop, as Forward Observation Officer, would go along with the company in the rear.

At 0630 hours we commenced with artillery fire, and at 0700 the companies crossed the start line. From the outset the tanks showed their mettle, and were into the woods well before the leading company. After

Captain Dennis Bishop, smiling in spite of it all!

a sharp battle the garrison was quickly defeated. They were good troops and fought very hard.

Then as the companies made their way into the objective, there arrived a tornado of shells. With the first concentration came tragedy. A report came in that Major Harry Lythgoe, Commander of B Company, was dead and two tanks had been hit. Then came the most unearthly

Track to the woods; Goch.

crashes outside our building, with flames and the smell of burning. The morning mist had lifted and our Battalion HQ was under observation from Weeze church, as was all movement to the woods.

I started to blanket the church with smoke shells, but they already had our range. Then came a frantic call from the leading company who found themselves in the centre of a counter attack. I had been a bit worried about Dennis, not having heard from him, but this call was very serious and removed all other thoughts from my mind.

The tank radio advised that the counter attack consisted of heavy shelling, followed by infantry and SP guns. There had been two more tank casualties.

This was a situation where the artillery officer really had to perform, and Battalion HQ was tensely silent as I called for priority on the air. Wireless discipline worked magnificently, the air became clear. I called for defensive fire (DF) as pre-arranged, then for mediums to deal with the SP guns. All this time bad news was coming in from the companies. I saw Colonel Brooke looking at me anxiously but not saying anything – and I prayed for more speed with the shells.

Opening barrage; Goch.

Reflect with me on those moments: the Battalion had got into the wood, but was being cut up by shelling. Now there was a counter attack. If that counter attack was allowed to get through, heaven knows what the cost to us would be. Whether the counter attack succeeded or did not was now my battle. Everything depended upon the speed and accuracy of the guns.

Suddenly, years later it felt – about four minutes in fact – a voice announced 'Ready on DF'. I shouted 'Fire', and the noise of battle was drowned by the roar of our guns.

A voice on the tank radio said, 'Can you go south 200 with the heavies'. I ordered the mediums 'south 200', and a laconic voice said, 'Good show – got him!' The leading company then reported the counter attack repelled and an SP gun on fire.

A few minutes later Dennis Bishop came on the air. He had set up an Observation Post but had been driven to ground by the shelling.

After a series of concentrations, food was sent down for the Battalion. Then the infantry radio told us that Major Alf Chaston, Commander of C Company, was badly wounded, Captain Lionel Purvis, Second in

25-pounder in action; Goch.

Command, had been killed, one of Dennis' signallers had been killed, as had two platoon commanders.

When Alf Chaston was brought back, I went over to the RAP (Regimental Aid Post) to see him. The pile of equipment outside bore mute testimony to our casualties, and when I went inside the number of injured was horrifying.

I wanted to go down to Dennis, and was in the street assessing the situation when a concentration of shells hit the road and surrounding buildings. A large chunk of masonry just missed me, but a tank officer was hit in the leg and a carrier smashed.

Then came a shout warning of another counter attack – my hands were full again. All that night it went on, with a stream of casualties coming back. The 4th Welch passed through us later in the night and got into the piece of wood ahead, where they proceeded to share our fate.

We had a sleepless night. At about 1100 hours, I left Battalion HQ and made my way down to the wood in a carrier. There was a faint sun and as I went, Typhoons (rocket-firing aircraft) came over with a mighty roar and knocked down Weeze church.

As we drew near to the wood I could see about 30 or 40 figures apparently basking in the sun and getting some overdue rest. I remarked on it to the driver, who looked at me a bit queerly but said nothing. As we got closer it dawned on me that these men were indeed resting, but would never awake again.

Then came a screaming salvo and we raced for cover. I met up with Dennis and his crew – all wonderfully staunch and brave – having an absolute hell. Then I needed to get back as I was worried about Battalion HQ, but for four hours there was no interval in the shelling long enough for us to get into the carrier and away.

Need I describe more? For two more nights and three days, we endured, never sleeping, repelling counter attack after counter attack, until the enemy was forced back.

On 27 February we were relieved, and went back to Goch for a night. However it was a Battalion weaker by 200 men and two company commanders. The tank squadron which had rendered such magnificent service had lost 11 of their 18 tanks.

The following day, exhausted and nearly asleep, we were moved round to face Weeze from the other side of the river. We were in contact with the enemy but without actual fighting. The next few days we moved through the thick woods to the east of Weeze, then on 3 March we moved back into Goch.

That night the Squadron Commander of 13/18 Hussars appeared. This was a bad sign but we could not believe, worn out and weakened as we were, that Command would commit us to another battle. But they did.

On 4 March The Mons were moved to Geldern by TCV (Troop Carrying Vehicle). At 0645 on 5 March we passed through the East Lancs to attack up the main road to Alpon.

This whole business was another taste of hell. We were all so tired that keeping our eyes open was difficult. Our objective was to clear the main road to the end of the thick wood before Alpon, where we should meet the Americans on our right and the Guards on our left.

We succeeded in reaching our objective, but neither Americans nor

Guards turned up. We were heavily shelled all day trying to get up the road, then found a farmhouse for Battalion HQ. This was continuously shelled, then an SP gun came up and fired several rounds right through it. The Boche came around us during the night. It can readily be understood that – weary as we were – nobody slept!

On the morning of 6 March a round cheerful red face that I knew from another regiment in the early days appeared saying, 'Hello, Old Man! We have heard about the bloody time you have had.' I was so utterly weary that I gazed at him and said, 'Who are you?' Back came the answer, '52nd Division. We are relieving you!'

It did not seem possible that it could be true! For 28 continuous days we had fought, and been out of contact with the enemy for only one night. Only once had I had my clothes off, and for only one night had I not been always on alert in case of a call for fire. I could hardly believe it!

However by about 1600 hours the takeover was complete, and as I drove away a salvo of shells came over and hid my friend in smoke and dust.

There is little more to tell. 'Operation Veritable' was a success. The Hun was pushed back over the Rhine for all its length. We had created an endurance record for 21st Army Group.

The Infantry were taken to Brussels to recover and reform. The Gunners went back to Geldern to rest and prepare for the Crossing of the Rhine.

(The following article appeared in the UK Daily Herald, dated 12 March, 1945. It tells of the advance through the Reichswald Forest by the 53rd Welsh Division, of which The Mons and 497 Field Battery were part. Ed.)

'THEY FOUGHT NON-STOP FOR A MONTH'

'Victor Thompson tells the epic story of the 53rd Division:

They are sitting in the ruins of a German village trying to bask in the reluctant March sunshine. They are shaved and their boots are clean They have a large hot meal inside them, a great content in their minds.

They come from the Fifty-Third (Welsh) Division. If you have not heard of it and its notable deeds, that is entirely because Security has cautiously hidden its identity much longer than I think necessary.

Out here, however, the Fifty-Third is spoken of with deep respect, especially by the German paratroopers, the cream of the German Army, whom it has recently beaten.

Glory – and Death

And today, the ban being lifted, I can at last reveal that of all the tough fighting on the British and Canadian sector between the Maas and the Rhine, the most sustained was endured by the Fifty-Third Welsh.

And if we are to get the matter quite straight it must be said that English regiments are well represented in that division.

Other divisions were put in and did their task and were pulled out. There was plenty of glory – and of pain and death – for all. But the Welsh went in on the first day and stayed until the last, and from what I saw of them during that terrible month I know that no troops fought more gamely anywhere.

They went into action on that grey morning of February 8th with their ears deafened by our mighty barrage. They went straight into the grim Reischwald forest, and they knew already that the armour which might have made their task easier was bogged down, and that the aircraft which would have made it easier still were grounded in the mists.

Forty men were wounded in the first clash. Men of the Field Ambulance hand-carried the wounded, because the only available road was 'Chewing Gum Alley', a clinging morass that all of us who ever trod it will ever remember with loathing.

Meanwhile, the men of the 53rd were plunging deeper into the fortified forest – into the mud, into the enemy – and the Sappers kept a way to them open through the mud bath. Amphibious ducks and weasels were aiding them by taking up supplies and taking out the wounded through the floods to the north, and the front-liners slogged ahead deeper and deeper into the enemy's forest defences, fighting sometimes from tree to tree, halted often, but going back never.

Corporals as COs

Sometimes battalions were temporarily out of touch, sometimes corporals became commanding officers because all the officers were killed or wounded.

The artillery thunder by day and night was such as to make sleep impossible. Even when the Welsh finally burst out of the woods into the daylight again and had their first brief rest of less than a day, they were only 100 yards away from where shells were dropping.

They went on to Goch and finished the task that others had begun. I saw them there and although the paratroop opposition was still tough they were almost elated because they were out of the forest, out of 'Chewing Gum Alley'. They said to me 'Don't call us the Fifty-Third Welsh any more, Call us the Fifty-Third Woodland.'

There it was that Private A. Williams, of Ynysybwi, South Wales, told of the capture of a German colonel and his men.

'As I came up to search him for weapons,' he said, 'he must have thought I looked threatening, because he said: 'Are you an English gentleman?' I said, 'Of course I am – and a Welsh one too!'

Those Road Mines

There, too, Lieutenant A. Cowan, of 16 Scotsman Road, Toller-lane, Bradford talked of the huge problem facing the Sappers.

'In one stretch of two miles,' he said, 'Jerry had blown the road in seven places. The craters were huge, and there were more prepared charges which had failed to explode and which we had gingerly to remove.

These charges were composed of a hundred pounds of TNT, six feet underground, with a layer of shells on top of that and a layer of mines on top of that again. Still, we managed to get the road open and keep it working.'

They were still at it on St. David's Day, the day of the Welsh. Some of them found some leeks and wore them and went into action and died. The Scots alongside them saluted their comrades' day with bagpipes.

There were house-to-house fighting and counter-attacks. The paratroopers fought fanatically, but they had always finally to give best to the hard-fighting 53rd.

One German soldier came in to surrender, and said if we would let him go back he would bring 200 of his comrades. We took a chance. He returned with 20 others. He was told that was not enough. He went back again and came back with another 40.

Not many of the Germans surrendered, however. Most of them fought on in a way which we should describe as heroic if it had been on our side, but which, since it happened against us, is usually described as fanatical. Anyway, it was fierce – almost as fierce as the way the Welsh fought.

40 Miles of it

They made the first contact with the American spearhead probing up from the Ninth Army front, and it was right that they should have that honour. They had certainly paid for it with many dead and wounded.

They went on and on and it is only now, with the Rhine's left bank secured at last, that they are out of the battle.

They have foot-slogged 40 miles in a month. Fighting for every yard. They have fired 1,000,000 rounds of machine-gun ammunition alone. They have had the longest, bitterest sustained fighting of the war, and they are today very, very tired.

And yet, as they sit here in the ruins, drinking interminable mugs of tea, they seem, apart from that weariness, entirely unaffected by their experiences.

Man, it seems, can get used to anything, and always endure a little more. If there is any maximum of endurance, however, then the men of the 53rd who fought in Normandy and in the Ardennes and at s'Hertogenbosch have surely set it in the Rhineland.'

CHAPTER 18
CROSSING OF THE RHINE
23 MARCH 1945

Following the conclusion of 'Operation Veritable', the Battery was put into a cluster of small farms, where they could rest, clean up and get everything ship-shape for whatever might be in store next. Meanwhile The Mons were moved near to Brussels to do the same thing.

Most officers and a large number of other ranks were able to get a short leave during this period. I went off to Brussels and had a colossal beat-up for 48 hours.

The only part of 53rd Division to be involved in the assault crossing of the Rhine was the artillery. Indeed I was grateful that we were to play a role in such a significant event. When I returned on 14 March, decisions were being made on the positions our batteries would occupy to support the crossing.

For the next few days we made our preparations either under cover of darkness, or by day under cover of the all enveloping smokescreen which shrouded about 60 miles of the Rhine bank.

First we did a general recce to find suitable battery sites, then gunpits were dug and carefully camouflaged. On the night of 21 March, the guns were taken into the area and hidden in farm buildings and barns. At last light on 23 March, the guns were put into their pits, zero lines recorded and sights tested. The fireplan had been completed, ammunition brought up and dumped, and there was an uncanny hush at about 1900 hours. The stage was set, the cast was ready, and the curtain had only to be rung up.

Our position was near the village of Gest, at a bend in the Rhine. We were some two miles from Wesel, which was on the far side of the river

Majors Hughes and Chessels before Rhine crossing.

and plainly visible. At 1600 hours on 23 March, there had been a heavy bomber raid in great strength on the town and a large number of 10 ton bombs were dropped. From where we were the ground shuddered and shook, and the bombs sounded like express trains as they fell. We were told this raid would be repeated at 2200 hours. It came dead on time, preceded by Pathfinders. Life must have been pretty grim in Wesel that night!

At 2130 the artillery barrage started – it was impossible to hear oneself speak, with the roar of guns and sound of shells shrieking overhead.

Wesel after two visits from RAF Lancaster bombers.

Commandos crossed the river first, then the infantry divisions. The Americans were doing a similar job to our right. At about 0200, it became quieter and we received a report that all was going well.

The next morning at 0930 we started firing again, and at 1000 an enormous air armada came over. Unfortunately the day was misty so we could not observe the actual dropping of the airborne forces. They met a certain amount of resistance and a number of planes flew back over our heads on fire. The crew of a Liberator bailed out and landed all over our gun position. We looked after them – nice chaps, all American. When I asked them what we could do to help, they wanted to know the quickest way to get back to Ipswich, from where they had departed at 0830 that morning!

Everything continued according to plan, and by the night of 24 March a bridge over the Rhine had been completed.

On 25 March we got the news that Major Chessels, our Artillery Second in Command, had been promoted to Lt. Colonel and posted to command a medium regiment.

My Battery was ordered to rejoin The Mons and cross the Rhine into Germany that same night.

And so the last great barrier was broken down, and 'Operation Eclipse' was about to commence.

CHAPTER 19

'OPERATION ECLIPSE' FINAL PUSH THROUGH GERMANY

25 MARCH TO 5 MAY 1945

*N*ow that the hurdle of the Rhine was behind them, the Allies commenced 'Operation Eclipse' – the complete elimination of the German Armed Forces.

It was a sunny, dusty day on 25 March when Joss Martin, Dennis Bishop and I went off to find The Mons at Kevelaer, just south of their old battleground of Weeze. We were made very welcome – rather like the Prodigal Sons – and a bottle of champagne was opened at once!

We moved off as a battalion column about 2200 hours, and were to cross the Rhine over a Bailey bridge which had been erected near the town of Xanten. The Hun had been using aircraft a great deal in attempts to destroy this bridge, and had nearly succeeded two or three times.

Our arrival in Xanten coincided with an air attack. An enormous anti-aircraft barrage went up, and huge chunks of metal rained down. We were parked in the street and this was most unpleasant.

In due course we moved up to the Rhine and to the bridge itself. It was just a plain platform on pontoons, but to everyone's relief we made an uneventful crossing.

Our concentration area on the other side was a small wood. All around were parachutes, gliders, containers and so on from the 6th Airborne Division's landing, together with a lot of debris from their battle the previous day. It was simply stunning to see the massive amount of equipment necessary to carry out such an airborne assault.

That night we moved towards Dingden, then received orders to attack and take Bocholt. Here there was an important road junction,

Temporary bridge over Rhine.

and it was essential to clear the town quickly to develop a bridgehead over the river which ran through it.

There is little to note in this attack. Put in by night after an initial artillery barrage, it was slow and very messy, as always with fighting in a town. However the south side up to the river was secured in due course, for some six casualties.

There were Boche on the far side of the river making themselves objectionable, so on 29 March we were ordered to get over and clear the north side of Bocholt. This was done by going into 71st Brigade's area and crossing over a bridge they had secured intact. The operation was complete by 1700 hours and the whole town was ours.

German civilians were then pulled out of cellars and shelters, and made to remove road blocks so that our armour could be launched for a breakthrough.

The following night we were ordered to join with 4th Armoured Brigade, and advance with them through Rhede. We were mounted in TCVs (troop carrying vehicles) and went 'swanning' (World War II term for armoured vehicles and tanks cruising about the countryside) which was wonderful! I was told to go along with The Mons as their

Bocholt after the battle.

artillery representative, and off we went. There was no resistance and we rolled along happily.

Our route took us through Borken, then we turned up a minor road towards the village of Oding on the Dutch frontier. In fact we did not get to Oding because the 7th Armoured Division were having a battle with some odd Huns along our path. We waited but it seemed unlikely that they would finish before nightfall, so the 4th Armoured Brigade laagered where they were.

The following day we went ahead to Oding, then over the border to Winterswijk in Holland. What a relief to be with people who smiled and were pleased to see us! What a pleasure to give chocolate and sweets to the children who ran up, laughing! In years past, the Dutch may have cursed the 'Yeomen of England', but not on 31 March, 1945!

Just as we were getting used to the idea of racing along with the Armoured Brigade, orders came for us to rejoin 160 Brigade near Vreden. This we did, early on 1 April.

We were very uncomfortable in a filthy farmhouse, so when we were warned to expect a move to Gronau I decided to be clever and go in advance with the Brigade recce party. I had no business to do this, so

Major Hughes 'swanning' with Armoured Corps; Germany.

when in the middle of the night all the recce parties were ordered to rejoin their battalions, I had a most uncomfortable time driving in the pitch dark and pouring rain to catch up with our group – a perfect token for April Fools Day!

On 2 April we approached the area of Rheine. After several moves for position in this very fast moving affair, The Mons were ordered to attack and take the village of Salzbergen on 5 April. They were to be supported by a squadron of tanks of the Royal Scots Greys for this battle.

Colonel Brooke and I worked out a fireplan, and the attack was launched at 1600 hours. The tanks, I regret to say, were not up to their usual standard and hindered rather than helped. They were engaged by some dug-in 20 mm anti-aircraft guns, and when one tank was knocked out the squadron commander said he wished to pull back. For the first time Colonel Brooke told them to leave, realizing we were not going to be helped by this particular tank squadron.

We regrouped and worked out another fireplan. Then the Battalion went in, with Joss as artillery Forward Observation Officer. The Germans fought well but by 2100 the Battalion was on its objectives, and Salzbergen was reported clear of enemy by 0630. A number of prisoners were taken.

During the battle our troops were troubled by a wandering SP gun, so I called for some Medium Guns and had several shots. The following day a patrol discovered the SP knocked out, a medium shell having landed inside it. I felt I had given value.

On 7 April we moved again, and went into the role of protecting the bridgehead over the River Ems at Rheine. A bloody battle for Ibbenburen was being fought by 71st Brigade nearby.

On the 8th we were ordered to do a long move up through the 7th Armoured Division, and reach the River Weser at Hiltrop. This move was uneventful. As we motored through Germany in the warm spring sunshine with young green leaves sprouting on the trees, it seemed strange that the people peering through curtained windows were our enemies.

Major Hughes' personal arsenal.

Colonel Brooke and I made a precautionary fireplan to cover our entry into Hiltrop and a battle plan was drafted. However all was quiet and peaceful, and an unopposed arrival was our good fortune.

At first light we set up an Observation Post in a church tower, with Dennis as FOO. I went to look over the Weser. This was the same river into which the Pied Piper had led the rats, many many years ago. In some way we were emulating the Pied Piper, except that we were driving the 'rats', and unfortunately too many were getting away alive!

A bridge had been built over the Weser at Hoya. On 10 April The Mons were ordered to move up, cross the bridge, and go south to Nienberg. The war was moving fast!!

After one night in Nienberg we pulled out at 0500 and moved towards the River Aller for the battle to capture Rethem.

Rethem 11 April 1945
At 1200 hours I went to the 'O' Group meeting, held to plan the coming battle.

Captains Bishop and Martin with Major Hughes by OP carrier; Hiltrop.

Pistol practice: Captains Thomson, H. Holmes, G. Davies, D. Bishop.

The overall Divisional objective was to achieve the capture of Rethem and Verden. This would open the corridor for our troops and armour to pour quickly through towards Bremen and Hamburg.

Rethem was a small town, but of strategic importance as it was situated on a major east-west road which crossed the River Aller at one of the few bridges in the area. It was essential to gain control of this bridgehead.

The Mons were ordered to capture Rethem.

The 5th Welch had attempted its capture the previous day. After a very unpleasant battle where repeated attacks were repelled, that battalion had withdrawn. Further, a soldier who had been captured and escaped reported that fifteen of our prisoners and others had been shot in cold blood. That this report was utterly false did not become apparent until some weeks later when all the 'murdered' men were found in a PoW camp.

Nevertheless that was the report, and as far as we knew the Hun in Rethem was taking no prisoners. It was therefore in a grim atmosphere that our battle plans were made.

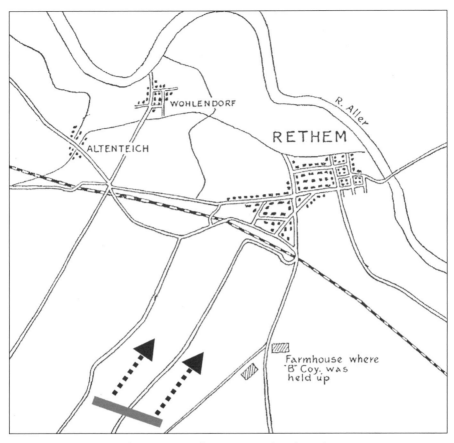

Action at Rethem on 11 April 1945.

Intelligence estimated that Rethem was defended by up to 1,000 marines. Also some super-heavy railway guns were in place.

We had a fairly large amount of artillery available to us. Regardless of how the Hun reacted, we were going to need it because our advance to the town meant crossing about one and a half miles of flat, open country, all in full view of the enemy. So apart from any normal shelling that had to be done, a fairly extensive smoke screen was going to be required to conceal our troops.

Across our approach to the town ran a railway line. It seemed reasonable to assume that there would be a line of resistance at or around that area. I therefore arranged for six Medium regiments to 'treat' the

Rethem; The attack was across this field with heavy railway guns at far side.

railway for 15 minutes. As part of the fireplan I ordered 2,000 rounds of smoke shells (this was in short supply and rationed due to our rapid advance, and was all I was allocated) and set the line of the smoke screens. On returning to Battalion HQ, I briefed Joss and Dennis, and detailed the latter as Forward Observation Officer to go in with B Company.

At 1630 the attack commenced. On the way in I found myself wondering 'Will it never end?' However those reflections never did any good and I dismissed them quickly.

The smoke started thinly, and down came the Mediums. I could see through my binoculars the flashes as the shells burst along the railway line, and also some other explosions.

The infantry went forward accompanied by tanks, but after half an hour it was plain that things were not going well. Resistance was stubborn and B Company was brought to a halt with our troops some 20 yards from the railway line. They were lying completely in the open, being picked off one after another. The tanks pressed in with total disregard for their own safety, and after running out of ammunition, drove up to the Hun positions and threw hand grenades out.

Captains Joss Martin and Dennis Bishop.

After some two hours the town was blazing. However our smoke supplies were getting dangerously low. I called urgently to Colonel Gore, my Artillery CO, and advised that we would have a disaster if we could not get our hands on more smoke shells urgently. Apparently my CO, the RASC, and those at the guns did a magnificent job to help. Ultimately I fired nearly 3,500 rounds – I was told stories of jeeps rushing to neighbouring regiments in the night and begging for smoke shells.

The battle was bitter and bloody. D Company on our left was also stopped and at an impasse. About 0200 hours Colonel Brooke decided to pull back a bit and think again. I had to juggle the smoke and bring it very close to our troops to help them move out, but this apparently worked.

We knew we had inflicted pretty heavy casualties on the Hun and we had taken about 60 prisoners. While our troops were coming back, I again leathered the town with medium, heavy and field artillery, with one thought in mind – Kill! Kill! Kill!

Railway guns did not fire. Note dead German in ditch in foreground.

At 0430 came a mighty explosion from the town – we assumed that the Germans had blown the bridge and were probably withdrawing. At 0700 a cautious patrol was sent forward and was not fired upon. Then the tanks came back to say they had prodded from the right and met only Boche who wished to surrender. Immediately Colonel Brooke sent a patrol forward and some 140 enemy put their hands up.

Despite the fact that we had pulled back during the night, the enemy had obviously been so severely punished that he had withdrawn. The Battalion was able to occupy Rethem at first light without opposition. This had been a very costly battle for The Mons, with some 40 casualties. However apart from securing a vital bridgehead, it had decimated a valuable German fighting unit at a time when all their resources were in critical need.

The town was totally devastated and littered with German dead. When the company commanders came in during the battle, they had reported that there were five large railway guns on the track, all swung

Rethem after the battle.

out against us but not firing. I inspected these guns when I got into the town. They were 105 mm Anti-Aircraft guns, and every one had been smashed by our shells. The dead all around testified to how ready they had been to open fire when my Mediums, bless them, came down.

The Sappers (engineers) wasted no time in starting to build a bridge across the Aller, but were shelled while they worked. On Friday 13 April the General came to visit and chatted to the troops.

That evening The Mons were ordered to move out, cross the Aller and prepare for another battle. Understandably we were all getting very weary: Drive on – Attack – Drive on!!! Will it never end????

Final Advance to Hamburg 14 April, 1945

We moved hurriedly during the night towards Atersen. There was a full blooded German counter attack under way against 71st Brigade and we were required to stop the enemy penetrating in our direction. By the morning of 14th the line had been held.

There had been some confusion during this advance, but after being awake night after night, everyone was bone weary and it was hard to get our faculties to register. And we were promised a rest – but only when Verden had fallen! In the meantime there was no let-up: Attack!!! Attack!!!

Rethem after the battle.

Our next objective, on 16 April, was to attack and take Kukenmoor and the woods surrounding the village. This was a dirty battle which was won at some cost. On this occasion we had a squadron of City of London Yeomanry tanks for support – they were first class. An interesting incident was encountering three American airmen who had been shot down and had lived in the woods for six weeks. They had trudged for many miles and could hardly believe that they had finally reached friends.

The following day we attacked the neighbouring village of Gohbeck and the surrounding area. We used guns and flamethrowers, which brought about a swift surrender after the initial clash.

On 17 April Verden was finally captured by other battalions. And so, with a sigh, we all settled down to sleep!

Bad news came on 18 April – Colonel Frank Brooke, our beloved CO, had been reassigned to 12th Corps. I say 'our' – I had lived such an intimate life with the man. Since September we had probably covered two lifetimes of experiences together. He came to the Battery to say Goodbye. It was with a very genuine lump in my throat that I wrung his hand and bade him farewell. Looked at calmly now, it should have been obvious that the war was nearly over. But at the time, desperately tired

Knocked-out German Panther tank.

and battle-weary, it was devastating to lose our trusted Commanding Officer.

In the interim, Major D.S.O. Bremner assumed command of the 2nd Battalion, the Monmouthshire Regiment pending the assignment of a new CO in due course.

On 19 April we moved via Walsrode to the area around Soltau, where there were pockets of enemy to be liquidated. This was the extremity of the Luneburg Forest, destined shortly to be the scene of the German surrender. During this journey came a sight that seemed to make it all worthwhile – lorry after lorry coming back laden with freed Allied PoWs. All of them were beaming and singing – it brightened one's heart to see them. But this was no time to ponder – turn north again, on to the Kill!

The neutralisation of the Soltau pocket was followed over the next few days by assaults at Behringen, Bispingen, and Topingen. All these were messy as this was mostly forest, which is always a rotten sort of war. Hundreds of prisoners were taken during the course of these operations.

Colonel Brooke saying goodbye; Verdun.

On 24 April we moved to Westerholz in the Rotenburg Forest. We attacked at 0100 hours, and filtered forward into the forest against opposition which gradually melted. By 26th we had cleared the woods. Hidden in this forest were thousands and thousands of searchlights, all parked close together and every one methodically wrecked.

At 2300 hours on 26 April we attacked the village of Hoperhofen and occupied it by 0500.

On 28 April the radio reported talk of Himmler's peace offer. Could it be true???

On 29th we made a long move to Quarrendorf, near Harburg and the River Elbe. The radio confirmed the peace offer to Count Bernadotte.

On 30th we moved again, this time to Borstel. The 4th Welch were to occupy positions on the Elbe, with The Mons in reserve. During the journey we were machine gunned by five FW-190 aircraft. This was a most unpleasant experience but there was nothing to do but wait it out. On arrival at our destination I went over to our OP on the Elbe – we could clearly see the towers of Hamburg in the distance.

1 May brought the news that Admiral Donitz had announced the death of Adolf Hitler. Surely it must be nearly over now?????

More exciting news came the following day. The Huns were negotiating the surrender of Hamburg. But even better was the order forbidding gunfire within five miles of the main road from Hamburg to the bridge over the Elbe. We were on the main road to Luneburg where 21st Army Group HQ was situated, and a number of cars went past with high ranking German army and navy officers.

3 May – the waiting was getting very tense!

On 4 May The Mons were moved into Harburg. There they found a lovely place for Battalion HQ. On the way there I met Colonel Brooke who said that Admiral Freiburg was negotiating something very big.

After dumping our kit, Jimmy Forsyth and I went to the lounge. I turned on a wireless set on the sideboard. After a moments silence it said, 'Here is a very important announcement. Earlier today all the German forces in North and Northwest Europe facing 21st Army Group surrendered unconditionally to Field Marshal Montgomery.'

Jimmy, Jerry Weiss and I gazed at each other. At last it was over!

Never again would I hear that frantic call for 'Sheldrake!!'

Never again in this theatre would our guns shriek their 'Death Song'.

Never again! Never again!

From the Normandy beach in June, 1944 to Harburg in May, 1945, this finally was Journey's End!

A WORD FROM THE MONS

The following extract is taken from the final chapter of the book:

History of The South Wales Borderers and The Monmouthshire
Regiment Part III, The Second Battalion The Monmouthshire Regiment
By Lt Col G.A. Brett, DSO, OBE, MC

The Gunners

No story of the 2nd Monmouths would be complete without a tribute to the gunners who had supported them in every action. 497 (Panteg) Battery of 133rd Field Regiment, Royal Artillery, was affiliated to the Battalion, and training in Ireland and England had brought the units into the closest companionship, which was cemented by their acting together in nearly forty engagements, great and small. Throughout all these actions, the speed and accuracy with which any call for fire was answered bred in the infantry complete confidence that, whatever happened, 'the Gunners would compete'. And compete they did: often firing concentrations 100 yards in front of the forward platoons, sometimes beating off counter-attacks by skilful and timely defensive fire, and always ready to give the utmost support at any time and in any conditions.

The men serving the guns and bringing up the ammunition were in the nature of things not known to the Battalion, but it is due to the Royal Regiment to give the names of those whom the 2nd Monmouths constantly saw in action. With Major R. Hughes, MC, the Battery Commander (known familiarly as 'One-five-Charlie') were Bdr. Harris, L/Bdr. McNally, Fetter and Wheater and Gnr. Young. With Captain D. Thomson, later relieved by Captain D. Bishop, DCM, were Bdr. Jopling and Gnr. McGeoch. Others were Sgt. Passmore, Bdr. Rush, Sgt. Simpson, Gnr. Lister and L/Bdr. Dickson who was killed in action near Goch. To all of them and to those at the guns, the Battalion now says: 'Thank You'.

The Battery's Guns at Harburg after the German surrender.

A TRIBUTE FROM THE MONS

The following letter was sent from Major H.J. Jourdain, MC, commander of 'B' Company to Major Hughes on 8 May, 1945:

'To. Officer Commanding 497 Battery. 133 Field Regt. RA. From. O.C. 'B' Coy. 2nd Bn. The Monmouthshire Regt.

Now that happier times have come I would like to send you on behalf of the officers, N.C.O.s and men of my Coy our heartfelt thanks for the Artillery support which we have had from 497 Battery through this long campaign. Whenever or wherever we have asked for fire support, it has been forthcoming, and more than that, it has been provided before we dreamt that we should need it.

Normandy, Voorheide, the Ardennes, the Reichwald, Rethem, and others are names which recall so much to us all. In all of them the faithful 497 backed us up until our 'Artillery Support' became taken for granted. We know what hard work was entailed and are profoundly grateful for it.

You will no doubt receive many tributes of congratulation. This is one from a Rifle Company, which has had cause to need your support so often. I am sure that no unit has ever had such efficient backing as we have had.

Good luck to you all in the future, and thank you.

Harburg, 8th May, 1945 (Signed H.J.Jourdain, Major) VE Day O.C. 'B' Coy. 2nd. Bn. Mons Regt.'

Date — time of origin

071115B May 45

From 53 Welsh Div Arty

To   81 83 133 Fd Regts   71 A tk Regt   25 Lua Regt
      344 SL (ML) Bty

R&O 30 (•) CONFIDENTIAL (•) a rep of the GERMAN HIGH COMD signed the unconditional
surrender of all the GERMAN land sea and air forces in EUROPE to the ALLIED
EXPEDITION ARY FORCE and simultaneously to the SOVIET HIGH COMD at 0141 hrs central
European time 7 May under which all forces will cease active ops at 0001B 9 May (•)
effective immediately all offensive ops by Allied Expeditionary Force are to cease
and tps are to remain in present posns (•) moves involved in occupational duties
will continue (•) due to difficulties of comn there may be some delay in similar
orders reaching enemy tps so units will continue to take full def precautions (•)
NO repeat NO release will be made to the press pending an announcement by the heads
of the three governments (•) all infm

                IN CIPHER   PRIORITY

                F. Steelman   IMMEDIATE

German Surrender – Cable from High Command ordering ceasefire.

CHAPTER 20

POSTSCRIPT

BY THE EDITOR

*M*ajor Richard Hughes remained in Europe on occupation duties for some eighteen months following the end of hostilities. After de-commissioning of the artillery regiment, he spent much time in administrative duties in towns in Holland. He was repatriated and demobilised in early 1947.

By this time, Richard and Rosemary had two small children, Carole and Paul. Richard went back to his pre-war job as a surveyor and they moved into a suburban house in north London – obviously a huge adjustment for both after so many years of war. They soon decided that this lifestyle suited neither of them, so they looked for something more fulfilling, ideally where they could work together.

Richard's mother, Caroline, owned a successful haberdashery and drapery business in Harrow, which had prospered during the war. It was decided that Richard and Rosemary would start a branch of this business in Wembley. It was set up in a small shop on a busy road, not far from the famous stadium, and the family lived in a tiny flat upstairs. Together they ran the small retail business very successfully, and this was one of the happiest few years of their lives.

When Richard and Rosemary married the war had just started, so there had been little opportunity for a lavish honeymoon. However they did manage a weekend in Cornwall, and they loved the area. So in 1954, a plan was hatched with Caroline to sell both London shops, and move to a suitable business in south-west Cornwall.

They acquired a substantial department store in Penryn. Richard managed the company, Rosemary ran the ladies fashion department, and Caroline became a sleeping partner. This was a successful enterprise, but

Richard and Rosemary Hughes, Cornwall, 1972.

it entailed much administration and hard work plus constant financial worries. Around 1965, they were approached by a large retail chain with an acceptable offer, so the business was sold.

By this time their children had left home, and Richard and Rosemary looked for a new challenge. They had been considering the hotel business for some time, as they had always enjoyed working together with minimal staff, Rosemary had a wonderful personality for guest relations, and Richard had always had a love for cooking. So they managed to acquire a delightful holiday guest-house in Falmouth. They operated 'Somerdale Hotel' for some ten years, working hard during the season but thoroughly enjoying themselves.

When they finally sold the hotel, their family had dispersed. Carole, now a medical doctor, had married an American heart surgeon and lived in Los Angeles. Paul had also become a rolling stone, and was then residing in New Zealand. In 1978, after Richard's mother had passed away, they made the somewhat courageous decision at their age to emigrate to USA. They settled in Santa Monica, close to Carole and

Richard and Rosemary Hughes, California, 1984.

their four grandsons, and enjoyed the wonderful Southern California climate and lifestyle.

Richard passed away in Los Angeles on 3 February, 1998, at age 84. Rosemary lived for another eleven years, travelling the world at a grand age to visit family and friends. She passed away on 29 July, 2009 also in California, at 92.

The war undoubtedly left an indelible impression on Richard Hughes. Obviously it could never have been an enjoyable experience. But coming from a suburban Victorian family with limited expectations, it was probably the first time in his life that he had been given any significant responsibility and recognition. He discovered that he had the ability to lead and function efficiently under extreme circumstances. While not necessarily the high point of his life, his war was obviously pivotal and a most profound experience. That he was able to discharge his duties so effectively and successfully would have given him justifiable satisfaction, and his wartime experience would have provided a lofty benchmark for whatever life had in store for him thereafter.

APPENDIX 1
MILITARY CROSS AND THE KING'S LETTER

BUCKINGHAM PALACE.

I greatly regret that I am
unable to give you personally the
award which you have so well earned.
I now send it to you with
my congratulations and my best
wishes for your future happiness.

George R.I.

Major R. Hughes, M.C.,
    Royal Regiment of Artillery.

APPENDIX 2
MENTION IN DESPATCHES
MARCH 1945, REICHSWALD CAMPAIGN

By the KING'S Order the name of
Major (temp) (Quarter-Master) R. Hughes, M.C.,
Royal Artillery,
was published in the London Gazette on
22 March, 1945,
as mentioned in a Despatch for distinguished service.
I am charged to record
His Majesty's high appreciation.

Secretary of State for War

APPENDIX 3
497 FIELD BATTERY, ROYAL ARTILLERY

(The following is a copy of a newspaper article found with Major Hughes' effects. Source and date unknown. Ed.)

'This week sees the ending of 497 Battery, 133rd Field Regt. due to the Regt. closing up to two Batteries instead of three. The Battery was first formed in Ireland in February 1941. It was mainly composed of B troop 331 Battery and personnel from 332 Battery, and was commanded by Major R. Simmonds.

After its initial formation in Portadown it moved in the early summer to Lough Brickland where its main task was to knit itself into solid form capable of operating as a Battery with efficiency and goodwill as its basis.

When the Regiment left Ireland in Nov 1941 the Battery moved with it to Monmouth. This was the home county of the Territorial Regt. and in this way for short periods many old members were able to see something of their families. Training continued; the main object still being to encourage and create that vital and necessary esprit de corps. In this the Battery was succeeding magnificently until it suffered the sad blow in the loss of Major Simmonds.

On its moving to Kent in April 1942 it was commanded by Major Wightman. All ranks having worked so hard to build up the spirit of the Battery it now seemed destined to have three different Commanders in a short space of six months. As everyone knows this is the most difficult thing for any unit to survive without losing much of the good work that has gone into its making. Major Wightman fell seriously ill and was never again able to be fully physically fit. He was followed by Major

Bolland, who after a very short stay also became ill and was invalided out of the Army.

In Nov 1942 Major R. Hughes was posted to the Battery from 132 Field Regt. At that time the Battery was stationed at Hucking, which as all who had anything to do with it will remember with apprehension and distaste, it being known as the 'mud heap at the top of the hill'. However Major Hughes set about pulling the Battery together, fighting all opposition whether geographical or military, with the one aim of making 497 Battery fully recognised and respected by all and sundry as a Battery which could always be relied upon to do a job well. That he succeeded in this there can be no shadow of doubt. Training and preparation went ahead; schemes were undertaken and during this essential period the Battery got to know the infantry whom it would support throughout the coming battle. They were the Second Battalion of the Monmouthshire Regt. commanded at that time by Lt. Col. W. Kempster. Never could any Gunner Battery have asked for a better, happier or easier Battalion with whom to work in action.

The months preceding 6 June, 1944 the Battery was stationed at Herne Bay and during that spring and early summer the members could be seen indulging in almost every form of exercise calculated to render them in a state commonly referred to as fit as a fiddle; marching five miles in 40 minutes, early P.T., running up and down the cliffs like peculiar gazelles, etc. This meant that when the great day dawned, at least they were mentally and physically prepared for whatever lay ahead, a fact for which they were to feel very gladly in those first harrowing days of Normandy.

The Battery landed in Normandy with the remainder of the Regt. and Division. For me to describe or add to what so many others, better qualified than I, have said of those first dust and sweat ridden weeks is unnecessary. It seems in fact the story of the Battery from here on is nearly the story of the Division and that has already been told. However there are one or two things which must be mentioned: such as having lost Col. Kempster; the good luck in finding the new commander Lt. Col. Brooke, DSO, so ideal, so capable, so efficient, and so charming;

the sad loss on Hill 112 of Sgt. 'Snowy' Davis; the tragedy of Lt. Arthur Stear on the drive to Arnhem; the so well earned M.C. for the Battery's Commander, Major Hughes; and many other incidents both tragic and proud which could be mentioned if this were to be a book.

In short what can be said is the hours of training spent in building both military efficiency and that so essential esprit de corps were well spent, as was so clearly evinced in the whole-hearted respect, thanks, and appreciation given to the Battery by its affiliated infantry, not only from its gallant Commander but also from the Company Commanders right down to the plain footslogger.

This I feel is the highest test and the highest source of praise, a fact of which 497 Battery has been most justifiably proud. It was a regrettably short time after V.E. Day that the Battery's Guns, those which had served it so well while the war lasted, were handed in at Hamburg, and it was almost possible to detect the glisten of a tear in the eyes of such Nos. 1 as the never to be forgotten Stan Haggett or 'Smiler' Wink as they watched their guns disappear down the road on their last journey. Since then, occupational duties on the Dutch-German border have been the main call of the Battery, demobilization has taken away many of the well known and well loved faces. However it will not be without a slight tightening of the heart that those who are left and those who have gone realise that after five such glorious years during which the Battery has held its head high the name 497 is now about to pass back into the annals of the Army Archives, from which it first appeared in those uncertain and trying days of early 1941.'

APPENDIX 4
25 POUNDER FIELD GUN

*T*he 25 Pounder was the standard British Army field gun of World War II.

The Mk II, 25 Pounder QF (quick fire) was introduced in 1939, and was used by British and Commonwealth armies well into the 1960s.

It was a gun/howitzer, with a bore of 3.45 in (88 mm). It could fire a variety of ordnance. The shell and cartridge were loaded separately, increasing the options available. Maximum range was around 7.5 miles. The gun was frequently used with a distinctive muzzle brake, which reduced recoil and barrel lift.

The gun was readily towed by a four wheel drive tractor vehicle. It could be lowered on to its self-contained circular firing platform when ready for action, so that it could easily and quickly traverse a full 360 degrees. It travelled with a trailer, or limber, containing its ammunition.

Each gun had a crew of six, commanded by a sergeant. The Field Battery had eight 25 Pounders, in two troops of four. The gun had a rate of fire of up to 8 rounds per minute.

The 25 Pounder was generally considered the best artillery piece of the war. Although it did not fire a large projectile, its range, accuracy, high rate of fire, and ease of mobility made it a highly effective weapon.

Images on the following two pages courtesy of Australian Military Equipment Profiles, Vol. 1, Field Artillery, 1939–1945 by Michael K. Cecil.

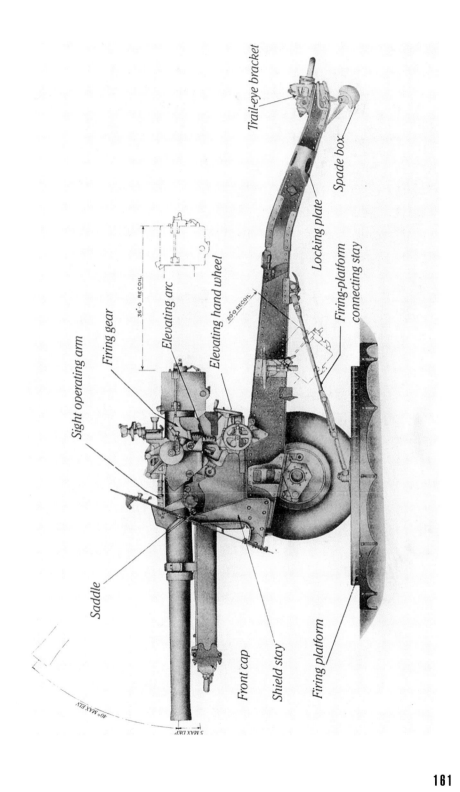

Trail-eye bracket

Spade box

Locking plate

Firing-platform
connecting stay

Sight operating arm

Firing gear

Elevating arc

Elevating hand wheel

Saddle

Front cap

Shield stay

Firing platform

36˙0 RECOIL

20·0 RECOIL

40° MAX ELEV.

5° MAX DEP.

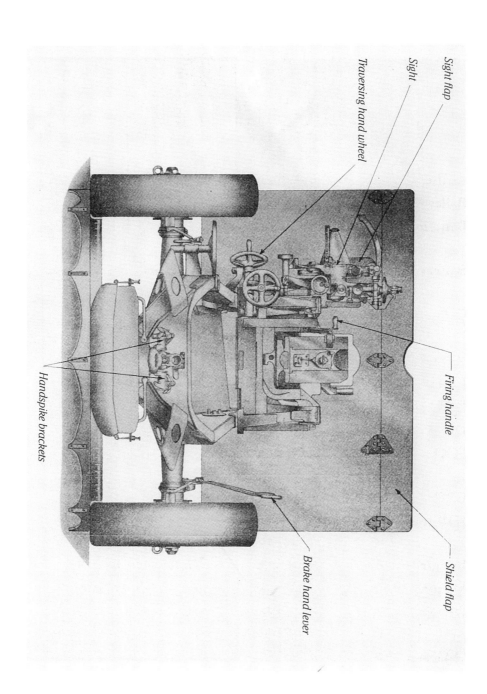

Sight flap

Sight

Traversing hand wheel

Firing handle

Shield flap

Handspike brackets

Brake hand lever

162

GLOSSARY 1
EXPLANATION OF SELECTED TERMS

Artillery	*Corps of army which uses large calibre guns*
Bailey Bridge	*A temporary floating bridge*
Battalion HQ	*Infantry CO's base, typically in a carrier, dug-out, or building*
Battery	*Artillery unit of eight 25 Pounder field guns and appr. 200 men*
CO	*Commanding officer*
Coy	*Abbreviation for infantry company, appr. 100 men*
CPO	*Command Post Officer (artillery)*
Crocodile	*Churchill tank modified for flame-throwing*
DCLI	*Duke of Cornwall's Light Infantry Battalion*
DF	*Defensive fire*
FOO	*Forward Observation Officer – Identifies targets for artillery fire*
GPO	*Gun Position Officer*
Half-track	*Vehicle with normal front wheels and tank-like tracks on the rear*
Infantry	*Foot soldiers, organised into Battalions*
Maquis	*French underground resistance organisation*
OP	*Observation Post – forward battery position for a FOO, typically in a high vantage point or carrier*
O-Group	*Orders Group – battle plan meeting at Brigade, Battalion, or Battery level*
One Five Charlie	*Major Hughes' wireless call-sign (and nick-name)*

PIAT	*Anti-tank shoulder-fired weapon, used by infantry*
RAP	*Regimental First Aid Post*
Recce Regt	*53rd Regt, Reconnaissance Corps (armoured)*
RHU	*Reinforcement Holding Unit*
RWF	*Royal Welsh Fusiliers*
RF 8	*Artillery tracked vehicle*
Sappers	*Engineers*
Sheldrake	*British Army wireless code to call the highest ranking artillery officer (or other rank) available at the radio location.*
Slit Trench	*One-man hole in the ground to provide shelter from shellfire*
SP 88mm	*German Self Propelled 88 mm Gun (reminiscent of a tank)*
Spandau	*German rapid fire machine gun*
Swanning	*Term for armoured vehicles and tanks cruising through countryside*
TAC	*Tactical Headquarters*
TCV	*Troop Carrying Vehicles*
The Mons	*Abbreviation for The 2nd Battalion, The Monmouthshire Regiment*
Tiger Tank	*Heavy German tank with 88 mm gun*
Typhoon	*Hawker fighter/bomber aircraft equipped with rockets for ground attack*
Wasp	*Carrier equipped with flame-throwing apparatus*
Weasel	*Amphibious transport vehicle*
'X'	*Battery Commander's identification pennant – normally flown on his half-track*
18 Set	*Manpack radio set weighing 34 lbs, with 4 mile range*
25 Pdr	*25 Pounder Field Gun*

DIVISIONAL INFANTRY AND ARTILLERY

Division	*Three Infantry Brigades and attached troops*
	Appr. 18,000 men
	Commanded by a Major General
Brigade	*Three Infantry Battalions and attached troops*
	Appr. 5,000 men
	Commanded by a Brigadier
Infantry Battalion	*Four Rifle Companies of appr. 100 men each*
	Appr. 1,000 men
	Commanded by a Lt. Colonel
Divisional Artillery	*Three Field Regiments and Anti-Tank Regiment*
	Commanded by a Brigadier
Field Regiment	*Three Field Batteries of 8 Guns each, plus transport*
	Commanded by a Lt. Colonel
Field Battery	*Two Troops of 4 Guns each. Plus command post,*
	technical, transport, and signal staff.
	Appr. 200 men
	Commanded by a Major

Other Artillery:

Medium Regiment	*Two Batteries of 8 x 5.5 inch Guns*
Heavy Regiment	*Two 4 Gun Batteries of 7.2 inch Howitzers,*
	plus Two 4 Gun Batteries of 155 mm Guns

GLOSSARY 3
53ʳᵈ WELSH DIVISION – ORDER OF BATTLE, 1944-1945

Infantry

71ˢᵗ Infantry Brigade

    1ˢᵗ Battalion, East Lancashire Regiment*

    1ˢᵗ Battalion, Oxford and Buckinghamshire Light Infantry

    1ˢᵗ Battalion, Highland Light Infantry

    4ᵗʰ Battalion, Royal Welsh Fusiliers*

158 Infantry Brigade

    4ᵗʰ Battalion, Royal Welsh Fusiliers*

    6ᵗʰ Battalion, Royal Welsh Fusiliers*

    7ᵗʰ Battalion, Royal Welsh Fusiliers

    1/5 Battalion, Welch Regiment*

    1ˢᵗ Battalion, East Lancashire Regiment*

160 Infantry Brigade

    2ⁿᵈ Battalion, The Monmouthshire Regiment

    4ᵗʰ Battalion, Welch Regiment*

    1/5 Battalion, Welch Regiment*

    6ᵗʰ Battalion, Royal Welsh Fusiliers*

Divisional Troops (Part)

81ˢᵗ Field Regiment, Royal Artillery

83ʳᵈ Field Regiment, Royal Artillery

133ʳᵈ Field Regiment, Royal Artillery**

71ˢᵗ Anti-Tank Regiment, Royal Artillery

53ʳᵈ Regiment, Reconnaissance Corps (Armoured Regt)

1ˢᵗ Battalion, Manchester Regiment (Machine Gun Regt)

* *These Battalions reassigned between Brigades during the campaign*
** *497 Field Battery was part of 133ʳᵈ Field Regt, RA*

ACKNOWLEDGMENTS

I am profoundly grateful for the assistance and advice I have received from many people during the production of this volume. In no particular order, I would like to specifically thank for their help Malcolm Naylor, Peter Summers, Ray Norman, Rusty Fitzgerald, Mansel Blackford, Randall & Suzie Blackford, Jonathan & Catherine Warn.

For turning my miscellaneous collection of documents and photographs into a finished book, I am indebted to:

- Kevin Long, of Page People Pty Ltd, Sunshine Beach, Qld
- Dan Kelly, of Watson Ferguson & Co, Brisbane, Qld

I have gained considerable background information about the campaign, and have included some extracts from the following publication:

- *History of the South Wales Borderers and the Monmouthshire Regiment, Part III, the 2nd Battalion the Monmouthshire Regiment, 1933-1952* By Lt. Col. G. A. Brett, DSO, OBE, MC

The basis of this volume is the personal wartime journal of Major Richard Hughes, MC. Photographs, newspaper articles, and various items were sourced from his own collection of memorabilia.

Finally I would like to thank my wife, Judy, for her ongoing encouragement and patience during the several years of preparation of this book.

Paul Hughes